W9-DGT-872

**SECTION
HANDBOOKS**

Introduction
to the Study
of Canon Law

2007

OTHER BOOKS BY THE SAME AUTHOR

- *Introducción al estudio del Derecho Canónico*, EUNSA.
- *Lecciones propedéuticas de Filosofía del Derecho*, 3ª ed., EUNSA.
- *Historia de la Ciencia del Derecho Natural*, 3ª ed., EUNSA.
- *Cuatro Lecciones de Derecho Natural*, 4ª ed., EUNSA.
- Una Caro. *Escritos sobre el matrimonio*, EUNSA.
- *Escritos de Derecho Natural*, 2ª ed., EUNSA.
- *Los eclesiasticistas ante un espectador*, 2ª ed., EUNSA.
- *Coloquios propedéuticos sobre el Derecho Canónico*, 2ª ed., Navarra de Ediciones.
- *Elementos de Derecho Constitucional Canónico*, 2ª ed., Navarra de Ediciones.
- Vetera et Nova. *Cuestiones de Derecho Canónico y afines (1958–1991)*, 2 vol., Servicio de Publicaciones de la Universidad de Navarra.
- *Pensamientos de un canonista en la hora presente*, 2ª ed., Navarra de Ediciones.
- *Pueblo cristiano y circunscripciones eclesiásticas*, Navarra de Ediciones.
- Vetera et Nova. *Cuestiones de Derecho Canónico y afines (1958–2004)*, 2ª edición remodelada, Navarra Grafíca Ediciones.

TRANSLATIONS

- *Critical Introduction to Natural Law*, Gratianus Series, Montréal, Wilson & Lafleur, 2006

  Introducción critica al Derecho Natural has also been translated into Italian (ed. Giuffré), French (éd. Biere), Portuguese (ed. Res Jurídica) and Hungarian (Szent István Táriulat).

- *Elementos de Derecho Constitucional Canónico* has been translated into Italian under the title *Diritto costituzionale canonico*, ed. Giuffré.

- A wide selection of "Una Caro" has been edited by ed. Giuffré under the title *Studi sull'essenza del matrimonio*.

SECTION HANDBOOKS

COLLECTION

Gratianus

SERIES

COFOUNDERS
ERNEST CAPARROS
MICHEL THÉRIAULT (†)

Introduction to the Study of Canon Law

Javier HERVADA

WILSON & LAFLEUR

2007

Bibliothèque et Archives nationales du Québec and Library and
Archives Canada cataloguing in publication

Hervada, Javier, 1934-
    Introduction to the Study of Canon Law (Gratianus series)
    Translation of: Introducción al estudio del derecho canónico.
    Includes bibliographical references and index.
    ISBN 978-2-89127-836-2

    1. Canon law — Study and teaching. I. Title.

KBR133.H4713 2007   262.9'40711   C2007-942395-7

English translation of *Introducción al estudio del Derecho canónico*, Pamplona,
EUNSA, 2007

Javier Hervada: E-mail: jhervada@unav.es / http:www.unav.es/canonico/j.hervada

Nihil obstat quominus imprimatur, Marianopoli, die 19ª Novembris 2007,
Michaël Parent, P.H., I.C.L., vicarius episcopalis, cancellarius,
Censor deputatus, Curiæ diocesanæ.

Imprimatur, Marianopoli, die 19ª Novembris 2007,
Ioannes Claudius cardinalis Turcotte, archiepiscopus Marianopolitanus,
N.P. 9/2007

ISBN 978-2-89127-836-2
Legal Deposit Bibliothèque et Archives nationales du Québec, 1st quarter, 2008
Legal Deposit Bibliothèque et Archives Canada, 1st quarter, 2008

Orders to:
Wilson & Lafleur Ltée
40, Notre-Dame Est
Montréal (Québec) Canada H2Y 1B9
Tel: 514 875-6326 / 1 800 363-3227
Fax: 514 875-8356
www.wilsonlafleur.com

USA:

www.CanonLawBooks.com
2662 East Allegheny Avenue
Philadelphia, PA 19134-5115
Tel: 215 634-2355
Fax: 215 634-2373

Midwest Theological Forum
1420 Davey Road
Woodridge, IL 60517 U.S.A
Tel: 630 739-9750
Fax: 630 739-9758
e-mail: mail@mwtf.org

Table of Contents

Presentation

This book is not an introduction to canon law in the strict sense, but rather an introduction *to its study*. It is intended then for those who are taking the first steps in its knowledge and, above all, to those who are starting to specialize in it through study and research. That is why at no time is the style informational; above all it requires an unhurried reading and, in more than a few cases, assumes that the reader has basic knowledge, be it canonical and juridical or theological or philosophical, and is always current with the documents of the Second Vatican Ecumenical Council.

This book covers two subject groups: the first subject is about the law of the People of God or the juridical dimension of the Church, and the second, about gnoseology and methodology. The first one answers the question, "What is canon law and what are its basic features?" while the other answers the question, "How can we know and interpret that law?" These are the two major subjects faced by the student of canon law. This book seeks to answer them in a synthetic style, as with most of the materials which came to light in other times[1]

---

1. Cf. J. HERVADA and P. LOMBARDÍA (†), *El Derecho del Pueblo de Dios*, I, *Introducción*, Pamplona, EUNSA, 1970, pp. 29–225; *Exegetical Commentary on the Code of Canon Law*, Á. MARZOA, J. MIRAS, R. RODRÍGUEZ-OCAÑA (eds.) (E. CAPARROS, General Editor, English Edition), Montréal/Chicago, Wilson & Lafleur/ MWTF, 2004, vol. I, pp. 1–119.

and are set forth here in an updated form. May the reader judge the success of this effort.

Dear reader, I leave this book in your hands in the hope that you find it useful.

Pamplona, October 7, 2006

I. THE JURIDICAL DIMENSION OF THE PEOPLE OF GOD

1. Introduction

Canon Law is the law of the Church. Law is a juridical system that organizes the social aspects of humankind. Because of its very nature there can be no law where there are no social relations or situations. A juridical system is also a dimension of social reality, to which the system is adapted and from which it receives the substantive principles that shape it. The character of each juridical system depends upon the nature and characteristics of the social environment governed by the system. For that reason the systematic organization, the content and the governing principles of canon law and its different branches should and do conform to how well the Church's social dimension and social structures are understood at each moment in time.

When the Const. *Lumen Gentium* presented to us the idea of the Church as it is presently understood—the fruit of meditating upon herself, as the Second Vatican Council was, according to Paul VI—it showed us an aspect of the Church that has long remained in the shadows in Catholic theology: the Church as the people of God. This analogy has deep biblical roots and has been used to bring out certain social aspects of being a Christian. To put it another way, it is a particular way of understanding the Church as a social group in the context of its larger mystery. Therefore, as a prerequisite to the study of canon law, it is a good idea to analyze the notion of the people of God and to ask what are its juridical dimensions and its characteristics.

2.   The People of God[2]

Lumen Gentium 9 expresses the notion of the Church as the people of God in the following terms: "At all times and in every race, anyone who fears God and does what is right has been acceptable to him (cf. Acts 10:35). He has, however, willed to make men holy and save them, not as individuals without any bond or link between them, but rather to make them into a people who might acknowledge him and serve him in holiness. He therefore chose the Israelite race to be his own people and established a covenant with it. He gradually instructed this people—in its history manifesting both himself and the decree of his will—and made it holy unto himself. All these things, however, happened as a preparation and figure of that new and perfect covenant which was to be ratified in Christ, and of the fuller revelation which was to be given through the word of God made flesh ... Christ instituted this new covenant, namely the new covenant in his blood (cf. 1 Cor. 11:25); he called a race made up of Jews and Gentiles which would be one, not according to the flesh, but in the Spirit, and this race would be the new people of God ... That messianic people has as its head Christ ... The state of this people is that of the dignity and freedom of the sons of God, in whose hearts the Holy Spirit dwells as in a temple. Its law is the new commandment to love as Christ loved us (cf. Jn 13:34). Its destiny is the kingdom of God which has been begun by God himself on earth and which must be further extended until it is brought to perfection by him at the end of time ..."

According to Catholic doctrine, raising a person to the supernatural order has a radical and total effect on the person as an individual and as a member of society. Just as in the natural order of things people are united among themselves by social bonds through the principle of sociality that is

---

2. Cf. also J. HERVADA, *Elementos de Derecho Constitucional Canónico*, Pamplona, EUNSA, 1987, pp. 42–46.

inherent in human nature, so also in the salvific order, Christians, who are persons regenerated in Christ, are related to each other by a connatural social dimension. This social dimension is ontologically inherent in a Christian and all Christians together form a social unit that is known under the name of the Church.

This idea has been traditionally admitted in the Church. It has been expressed in various ways, from Saint Paul's *Corpus Christi, quod est Ecclesia* or Tertullian's *Corpus de conscientia religionis* to *perfect society* in the doctrine of later centuries, or *people* by the Second Vatican Council. These different expressions are not incompatible with one another, nor can any one of them be substituted in total for any other. In addition to making the analogy of the Mystical Body, the Second Vatican Council used three different expressions—*people, society* and *community*—to refer in each case to different shades of meaning. The term *people*, however, is a basic notion with respect to the other two, which express two levels or modalities of the basic social unit, the people of God.

What is the meaning, then, that the Church's official and theological doctrine is trying to convey with the expression *people of God*? As Semmelroth[3] says, in using the term *people of God*, along with other theological aspects, the Church is trying to emphasize the following features: a) *Unity*: Above and beyond any diversity that can exist among them, the Christians form a single body. b) *Sociality*: We have alluded to this characteristic above. Christian faithful are not only a single entity, they are also integrated and related to each other by social bonds. c) *Equality*: Beyond any distinctions, there exists a fundamental level of equality among all the faithful which takes precedence over any differentiation. And d) *Historicity*: The Church is a social body with a historical existence as such; the Church exists through its bonds and

---

3. O. SEMMELROTH, "La Iglesia, nuevo Pueblo de Dios," in *La Iglesia del Vaticano II*, Spanish edition, I, Barcelona, 1966, pp. 451 ff.

purposes on both the atemporal and metahistorical level of divine realities and on the temporal (*time* dimension), historical and external level of human realities. The people of God, the Church, are the salvific Kingdom of God in the historical dimension of this world.

It is necessary to add here that the historical dimension of the people of God must be looked at according to its eschatological nature (*LG*, chapter VII). According to Christian teaching, the historical dimension of the Church is only a *phase* or *stage* in the life of the Church, which moves towards *consummation* or perfection in a new mode at the end of time. The eschatological dimension carries with it a sense of expiration and the ephemerality of the Church's existence in time, and in some sense that dimension is present in the Church's voyage through history. It colors the Church's evolution and causes a tension in it that impels it to achieve the maximum eschatological consummation possible in the present time. Because law belongs to the earthly dimension, in that sense it is an outdated dimension of the people of God. But at the same time it is, or should be, a historical way of achieving in the present the justice and peace that are proper to the Kingdom of God to be consummated at the end of time.

Still, without this group of features, we cannot properly speak of *people* in a sense which is analogous to what we understand as people in the human context. We would only be able to speak of people in the metaphorical sense. This group of features, however, is still not the principal characteristic features of the notion of the people of God. In today's language the word *people* has a whole range of diverse meanings. However, they are not an impossible obstacle to interpreting the meaning as applied to the Church because the expression *people of God* is understood as in the Biblical use of the word, in a sense similar to how it is applied and realized in the *People of Israel*. Accordingly, the Church is a People because of the following:

a) Its members enjoy unity of origin, with common personal and vital—ontological—traits that unite them and link them together; members of the Church share the same heritage. In a biblical context, peoples are considered to be formed by the union of families with a common bloodline. Abraham is head of the Chosen People, Ishmael is head of the Ishmaelites, Ammon is head of the Ammonites, and so forth. In the old people of God, Israel, bloodlines go back to the patriarchs, and in a special way to Abraham. In the new people of God, these blood links do not exist, but there are analogous supernatural bonds that are produced by insertion in Christ, in whose divine filiation the faithful may participate through grace. Christians have been made into God's children through grace and therefore they are *brothers* one to another (the bond of fraternity).

b) Because of this nature and its own virtuality, Christians are a *cohesive* group conscious of their unity in a way analogous to how it was in the biblical context—and still is today in the Middle East—with peoples based on the *ius sanguinis*. This solidarity is essentially manifested in the bond of charity, in which the community of affection and mutual responsibility (mutual help and responsibility on the salvific level) is rooted and should be carried out to its fullness. But solidarity is also rooted in unity of faith and goods in the supernatural order, especially the sacraments.

c) The people of God show a *unity of mission* and interests (still in the supernatural order) in the context of humanity. All the people of God, and not just the Church's hierarchical organization, have been brought together to continue Christ's mission and to be an *instrument* and *sign* of salvation and a *participant* in Christ's redemptive mission.

d) Like the People of Israel as was common in their cultural and historical context, the people of God are organized into a higher juridical unit. In the case of Israel and other peoples around them, the juridical unit was political; in the case of the Church, it is purely religious. In order to underline this characteristic, the Church has with varying degrees of correctness been called the perfect society, the primary juridical system of law, etc. All of those expressions, taken out of the cultural and historical context of the time when they were adopted, tend to accent the Church's characteristics as the superior juridical unit or body; the expressions therefore reflect the traits of an independent and juridically structured society analogous to the superior juridical units of the historical moment. This structuring as a superior juridical unit implies certain hierarchical phenomena without which it would not be possible for the Church to appear in the human context as an independent society of public law, analogous to organized, juridically superior societies. And indeed, the Church is structured not only as a community, but also as an organically formed society (*LG* 8). By the will of its Founder, it includes a hierarchy endowed with an authority that in its order—the supernatural order—is not only autonomous but *supreme*.

The analogy of the people of God points in particular to the external and historical aspect of the Church. But, as Catholic theology teaches, the Church has an internal element to which the figure of the *Mystical Body of Christ* makes special, although not exclusive, reference. This internal element also has cohesive relationships and unifying bonds; it is presided over by Christ, the invisible head of the Church, who, through the sanctifying action of his Spirit and his gifts and charisms, allows the faithful to participate in his divine life and leads them to their proper end. But the Church's external and internal elements form a single and unique reality. As Pius XII taught in the Enc. *Mystici Corporis* and *Lumen Gentium* has again repeated, the society endowed with hierarchical bodies and the Mystical Body of Christ, visible reunion and spiritual community, the Church on earth and the Church endowed with celestial goods are not to be considered as two different things. They form a complex reality made up of a human element and a divine element. In a profound analogy, the people of God are like the mystery of the Word incarnate (*LG* 8).

APPENDIX

Why do we say that the Church is the *New* People of God? If the Church is the New People of God, it necessarily occurs because, at the same time, it continues and replaces the Old People of God. There is an Old People of God, a true people united with God through the Alliance between Yahweh and Israel. Throughout the history of the Old People of God, only a *remnant* was always faithful to the Alliance, faced with so many infidelities of the leaders and the ordinary people of Israel. However, that Old People is not replaced *a radice* by another new one, but rather the New People of God is the transformation of the Old People towards its fullness or consummation (v. gr. the substitution of the blood ties by the bonds of grace). The Old People of God is present in the *remnant* of Israel, who believes in the Messiah, becomes a follower of Him—the Apostles, the disciples, and as many as believe in Jesus Christ—, receives his Word and, at the Pentecost, the Holy Spirit. With this *remnant* of Israel (the Apostles and the other disciples, with the eminent figure of the Virgin Mary), Christ establishes the New Alliance—which he carries out in the Easter mystery—, organizes a germ of the New People of God and edifies it definitively with the mission of the Holy Spirit. So then the New People of God is the *consummation or fulfillment* (taking to its fullness, according to the divine promise) of the Old People of Israel, which ceases to exist as this People of God, although it is still loved by God, because the divine gifts and the vocation are irrevocable (Rom. 11:29).

Therefore, it is obvious that the New People of God must continue to be the true People and maintain the features of a people, albeit transformed and completed. And the first and most fundamental, without which the rest would vanish, is the historicity, a religious community *in hoc sæculo*, with an existence, an organization and a structure characteristic of this world. Without forgetting, naturally, the internal element—constituting the essence and fundamental principle of its life and its action—then, the external element is where lies in particular the fact that the Church is the "people," the New People of God.[4]

3. Social Bonds

The people of God, who are the Church, are shaped by the social bonds among the members, and some of those bonds are juridical bonds. One characteristic of social bonds is that they are multiple; some appear in the strictly internal dimension of the Church, while others appear in the external dimension, and finally, some are common to both dimensions, although with subtle differences in each.

In the internal dimension the bonds of unity find one of their expressions in the relationship known by the term *communion of saints*, a community of spiritual goods. The community of faith and the bonds of charity are also reflected in the internal dimension.

In the people of God as an external social group appearing in the human historical context, in accordance with what has been said, we can distinguish various types of bonds. First there is the bond of fraternity, under which the members form a united community. This bond of unity may in turn be broken down into a community of faith, a community of worship, a community of purpose and the bonds of affection (mutual charity) that should preside over the relations among the faithful. Second, there is the hierarchical bond by which the members of the people of God are united in a relationship of authority with the proper pastors.

The Church, the people of God, therefore has a community dimension at the same time that it is organically structured by the hierarchical principle; there is a hierarchy in the Church that has capital functions granted by Christ himself.

---

4. Cf. Dogmatic const. *Lumen Gentium*, no. 9.

The set of social bonds is governed by three principles. First is the *principle of fundamental equality.* According to the Second Vatican Council, among the faithful there is a true equality with respect to human dignity and a common action to build up the Body of Christ (*LG* 32) i.e., with respect to the *fundamental condition* of the members of the people of God and to *actions*, common to all, that are directed toward achieving their end, which is the expansion of the Kingdom of God. The principle of equality has a double foundation: first, the common dignity and freedom inherent in the condition of being a Christian, a child of God (*LG* 9), or, what amounts to the same, the common dignity and freedom of a human being who is a participant in the divine filiation; second, the fact that because of being a Christian, every member of the faithful is a living and active member of the Church and is called upon to obtain the growth of the people of God and to collaborate in achieving the Church's ends (*LG* 33).

The second principle is the *principle of variety* in the path to follow and the manner of obtaining the ends of the people of God and of carrying out their activities. Under this principle falls the principle of the distinction of functions or ministries. Because of this, "By divine institution the holy Church is ordered and governed with a wonderful diversity" (*LG* 32). This principle signifies the deeply rooted and constitutional lawfulness—a lawfulness that cannot be violated without at the same time violating divine law—of the variety of rites, ways of life or apostolate, and it also signifies a necessary distinction among functions.

Finally, in certain spheres of activities and functions, the distinction is governed by the *institutional principle.* The people of God owe their deeply rooted existence to a divine convocation and an act of foundation by Jesus Christ, who is the true Head (*LG* 9). The people of God are, then, an institution (see *infra*, 4) whose fundamental traits were laid out by the Founder, and their history and development depend in the last analysis on divine action through His gifts (*LG* 4). The meaning of this for our purpose is that there are a number of activities and functions that are carried out by persons who do not receive the mission to fulfill them from the Christian community. Under this principle there are in the Church hierarchical functions, as we have stated, that carry with them the mission to exercise pastoral power in the service of the community and they are the framework of the entire institutional edifice of the people of God. In relation to hierarchical functions there is a *functional inequality* among the faithful. Above all, functional inequality indicates that these functions do not stem from the Christian people, but that the functions have been granted to the hierarchy directly by Christ. That is the consequence of the Church being an institution.

APPENDIX

The social bonds of the People of God, because of their particular configuration and nature, receive the name of *communio*. In this sense, it can be said that the Church is a *communion*. These bonds of *communio* are broken down into *communio fidelium*, or the communion of all the faithful among themselves, and the *communio hierarchica*, or communion with the hierarchy, based on the hierarchical principle, that is, on the structure formed by the *ordo—plebs* binominal.

Now then, the *communio* must be properly understood. If it is *communion*, it is because it is a matter of relationships based on the *caritas*, on the mutual affection, which involves living the unity among everyone. But it is not just love or affection. This is explained properly in the number 2 of *Preliminary Explanatory Note* of the Dogmatic constitution *Lumen Gentium*: "The idea of *communion* was highly valued in the early Church, as indeed it is today specially in the East. It is not to be understood as some vague sort of *goodwill*, but as *something organic* which calls for a juridical structure as well as being enkindled charity." So, then, it is an organic reality inspired by affection and love, but which requires a juridical form.

This means that the *communio fidelium* and the *communio hierarchica* must be imbued with charity; nevertheless, they are constituted as such through the juridical structure, through the relations of law or juridical relations, with true *potestas* and true *debitum* (what is just, what is owed).

The theses, such as that of Corecco, that "dejuridify" the *communio*, understanding it only as union and unity—although certainly binding—based on the *caritas*, are not, then, *consonant* with the *Preliminary explanatory* note of the Council. This has its basis on an ajuridical concept of the Church, meaning that justice in the Church is not the human justice of giving to each his right, what is his, but that it rather is divine justice, which is translated into the three theological virtues: faith, hope, and charity. If there is no justice of giving to each his right, there is no, strictly speaking, juridical dimension in the Church.

It should come as no surprise that in one of Corecco's writings he claims that one must obey the pontifical rules, but not because they come from a power of jurisdiction, but through the *communio*, that is, through the union and unity that proceeds from it as charity, that is, certainly, binding.

That is not the correct concept of *communio* which, as we have seen, requires a juridical form. The *communio fidelium* involves juridical relationships among the faithful, and the *communio hierarchica* is a reality based on the *sacra potestas*, of which jurisdiction or power of command of a juridical nature, which generates the strictly juridical duty to obey, is an unavoidable dimension.

With respect to the principles we examined in the text, we need only to insist that there are *three* principles, two of them referring to the condition of being a member of the faithful (equality and variety), while the third one refers to the hierarchical distinction, to the *ordo—plebs* binominal, which does not belong to the condition of the faithful, but to the hierarchical constitution of the Church (hierarchy—faithful relationship).

We say this because not infrequently there are some who reduce these principles to two: in variety they include the distinction of functions derived from the *ordo—plebs* structure. This is clearly a confusion. The hierarchical distinction of functions does not belong—obviously—to the condition of the faithful, while the principle of variety refers to the non-uniformity in the charisms, spirituality, forms of apostolate, etc., characteristic of the condition of the faithful.[5]

4. Institution and Community

The one people of God, since it is one, is a complex reality that is structured and organized according to two factors: the institutional factor and the community factor. Both reflect the Church's two-fold character as the *medium* or instrument of salvation and as the *fruit* or result of redemption (*institutum salutis* and *fructus salutis*, in the terms used by theologians).

Christ institutionalized the salvific media in the people of God, who are the sign and instrument of salvation. The sacraments and all media and aids to achieve salvation are found in the people of God. That is why the Church is an *institution*, born of a founding act by Christ. Fundamentally, the Church's structure and organization depend upon that founding act and not upon the will of the people who compose it.

In this respect, the term "institution" means a social group based upon a special founding act and placed in the service of a specific social task that transcends the particular interests of the people who serve it and that functions as an objective and permanent end for that group.

---

5. Cf. A. BANDERA, *La Iglesia misterio de comunión*, Salamanca, 1965; S. DIANICH, *La Chiesa mistero di comunione*, Torino, Marietti, 1975; J. HAMER, *L'Église est une communion*, Paris, Cerf, 1962; J. HERVADA, *Pensamientos de un canonista en la hora presente*, 2nd ed., Pamplona, EUNSA, 2004.

Inequality appears in a special way in the above-mentioned institutional factor because in relation to the means of salvation, a member of the faithful may be in different positions: as *minister* and *giver* of the means, i.e., as pastor, consecrating priest, etc. (hierarchic priesthood), or as *target* and *receiver*, offering community, etc. (common priesthood). Being a salvific institution, the Church is configured as an *organically established society*, presided over by the hierarchy. Within these institutional lines, the people of God appear with an organization of their salvific means before which the ministers are organized; the faithful are the targets of their activity. "In order to shepherd the people of God and to increase its numbers without cease," says the Second Vatican Council, "Christ the Lord set up in his Church a variety of offices which aim at the good of the whole body. The holders of office, who are invested with a sacred power, are, in fact, dedicated to promoting the interests of their brethren, so that all who belong to the people of God, and are consequently endowed with true Christian dignity, may, through their free and well-ordered efforts towards a common goal, attain to salvation." (*LG* 18)

At the same time the Church is the congregation or meeting (*ekklesia*) of the disciples of Christ, saved by Him. The Church is the group of men and women who have answered the call of God (*convocation*) and who, regenerated by grace and having become the children of God, meet or congregate through common bonds in a community of origin, goods and purpose that is presided over by the bond of charity and the principle of equality. The Church is the *fruit* of salvation, which also tends to be disseminated and intercommunicated (co-answerability, non-hierarchical apostolic action, Christian community of goods, etc.).

In this regard, we understand a community to be an organized social group in which there are, or at least predominate, unity of origin and of concord, which are manifested in common possessions and in common and hierarchical relationships.

An *institution* arises in the heart of a *community*. Thus it is not an issue of there being two separate levels or two watertight compartments. There are two intercommunicating factors that partake to a certain degree in each other. At the same time and in a complex unity, the people of God contain both institution and community as proper configurative dimensions.

APPENDIX

In recent times, a few writers have configured the Church as an institution differently. With varying nuances, in all of them, it is common to understand that the epoch of Christ and the Apostles was charismatic and that there was no institutionalization of the Church at this time. There was a shift from the charism to the institution with the successors of the Apostles in a gradual process of evolution, similar to what is noted in every human society, in which there is the phenomenon of the "objectification" of the charism and the resulting shift from the charismatic leadership (which is an extraordinary situation) to an institutionalized organization.

This is what would have occurred in the Church, whereby the "institution" in her would not have its origin in Christ, but rather in men; it would be a human work. This has a clear consequence: the divine law is not a law; canon law is a human product, the result of institutionalization; that is why, for them, only positive human law is law. Regarding this type of claims, it should be said that, although they are clever, they are not plausible.

Their exclusively charismatic vision of the primitive Church is usually based above all on the Pauline communities as, in their opinion, they appear in the Acts of the Apostles and in some passages of the epistles from the Apostle of the People. But it is a partial vision.

In the primitive communities, various charisms with an external projection can be observed—prophets, gift of tongues, gift of interpretation, doctors, etc. Nevertheless, with the same clarity, the said scriptural texts show us both those *resounding* charisms—so to speak—and an obvious institutionalization of the functions. They are not the charismatics whom the Apostles, and specifically Saint Paul, place at the head of the Christian communities, but rather they institute ministries, *episcopos* and *presbyteros* ministers; through something instituted by Christ (who instituted all the sacraments), which is the sacramental laying on of hands or the sacred ordination. The capital office—the office of government, oversight, correction, and custody of the deposit of the faith—does not come from a charism, but from a sacrament, which is *institutum*, institution and institution of Christ. In the Acts of the Apostles and in the Pauline epistles, the charisms are as evident as the institution. The institution does not proceed from an evolution of the charism; from the start it has its origin in the foundational Will of Christ and in the sacramental action—sacred ordination—of the Apostles.

Moreover, in order to explain the so-called shift from the charismatic Church to the institutionalized Church, the tenants of this opinion do not found it on prominent theologians and canonists—there are none—but on non-Catholic secular writers, philosophers, and sociologists who refer to the shift from charismatic secular personalities or leaders to the subsequent institution. They are authors who write, not on the Church, but on human, civil society; and they describe, therefore, a natural, social phenomenon. Perhaps the most quoted author is Max Weber, there being no lack of references to H. Shelsky, Summer, A. Gehlen, and others.

This involves falling into considerable confusion with the terms "charism" and "charismatic leadership" when they are characteristic of the People of God and when they are applied to human or civil society. In each case they signify distinct realities, and therefore these terms, used indiscriminately in each case, are no longer analogous, but misleading. In the Church, the charism is a gift of the Holy Spirit, a grace *gratis data*, not for one's own benefit, but for the good of others or for the Christian community. The charismatic leaders in the People of God are positions of pre-eminence or influence—consider, for example, Saint Catherine of Siena—roused by the Holy Spirit, and they have their origin in the *lex gratiæ*; they are supernatural gifts.

On the other hand, the so-called charismas in human and civil society—"having charisma"—and the resulting charismatic leaderships are very different things. A "charismatic leader" is a naturally attractive or "magnetic" personality, with an aura that causes a type of magnetization with people, groups, or even nations. All this is a natural phenomenon that has nothing to do with the grace of the Holy Spirit; it is a sociological phenomenon moved by the natural forces of human, secular, and civil sociality.

Therefore, the theses of the theologians and canonists under consideration are tainted at the root. The organizational evolution of the Church—upheld and guided by the action of the Holy Spirit—is completely different from the consolidation of the charismatic leaders of human society into institutions. They are two phenomena that cannot be adequately superimposed, and if one seeks to combine them, one errs.

With respect to the fact that the Magisterium of the Church has always defended the fact that the People of God are an institution *ab origine*, it is enough to recommend a reading of numbers 18 to 20 of the Dogmatic constitution *Lumen Gentium*.

5.   The Need for Law in the People of God

As we have just seen, the people of God are structured as an organization and a community by the will of Christ. This organization and community structure is "brought into operation through the sacraments and the exercise of virtues." (*LG* 11) In other words, the people of God are existentially realized by virtue of the dynamism which is inherent in the process of salvation—as it appears in today's economy of salvation—and in the Christian life. Organization is a dimension of those dynamics.

Indeed, through their own efficacy, some sacraments perform specific functions within the people of God. For example, by virtue of baptism the faithful are commissioned to participate actively in the life of the Church and to develop the seed of salvation received, with a specific apostolic vocation. Another example is the sacrament of orders by virtue of which a member of the faithful is destined for hierarchical functions to sanctify, teach and govern the people of God. The life of the Christian, guided and driven by the virtues, tends to be achieved by works and service to others. All of that is part of the rich variety of personal vocations and charismas.

Now all of the above postulates a social order in which the people of God can find its proper balance. That social order is canon law, which is not a superstructure with respect to the supernatural roots of the life of the people of God, since it is derived from and postulated by the faithful. Nor is it, nor should it be, a unilateral expression of the will of the hierarchy since, because of the exigencies of the divine constitution of the Church, canon law must ensure that there are spheres of autonomy, which are needed so that all the faithful may participate in ecclesial tasks. Canon law is not something limited to engendering duties of obedience, but a guardian of freedom and a way to act responsibly.

But the need for law in the Church should not be translated into simple convenience, strong though that may be. The juridical dimension is *necessary* because without it the Church is not comprehensible as it was founded by Christ. It is the essence of the Christian person, as well as the configuration and structuring of the Church, that inherently require justice, which must have a juridical dimension. Being incorporated into the Church, having a hierarchical position, receiving charisms, do not rest solely on charitable relationships among the faithful, nor on a duty or responsibility toward God. They fit into relations of solidarity and service that are based on the requirements of the faithful's condition with respect to other members of the Church and on the ministerial nature and function of the hierarchy. Thus they are relationships that involve justice and they inherently assume that there will be a juridical order.

So the fact that there is a juridical dimension to the people of God is not considered to be something that, if denied, merely implies a mistaken assessment of circumstances (assessment of the suitability or unsuitability of juridical norms). It is rather a truth about the nature of the people of God, who carry the evangelical message; if the juridical dimension is denied, it may mean denying the very revealed truth.

APPENDIX

A corollary to the theory of the shift from a charismatic time in the Church to an institutionalized one, such that the institutionalization of the Church would not have its origin in Christ, but would rather be a human process, is a denial of the need for law in the People of God. Thus we read in a book published in 2004: "There is no ontological nor theological need for the Church to have juridical rules of conduct."

We said it was a corollary of that theory. And, in fact, if it is understood that the first phase of the history of the Church was charismatic, there was no law in it; therefore, there is no divine law as a juridical dimension of the *Mysterium Ecclesiæ*, the Church is, in its intimate reality, ajuridical.

To the extent that the institutionalized Church, because it is an institution, is understood as a human work and, inasmuch as every human work is contingent, the Church *in history*—"historified"—would lack the necessary elements or factors, which would correspond to the metahistory, to the Church that transcends history. In this way, we come to the conclusion that there is no other law in history than positive (human) law, which is, by its nature, *contingent*, that is, it may or may not be, or may be one way or another. Years ago Corecco claimed that the institutionalization of the Church does not necessarily require juridicity, because it may also have been structured charismatically.

Given that this set of assertions is a corollary to a thesis that is not correct—that of the shift from charism to the human institutionalization—, it cannot be accepted either. The Church is institutionalized by Christ, by divine law, which is in history as the true law and as a *necessary* dimension of the external element of the Church. It is the Catholic doctrine of the *Ecclesia Iuris*, from which is deduced number 16 of the decree *Optatam totius* when it says that *in iure canonico exponendo* [...] *respiciatur ad Mysterium Ecclesiæ*, which would not make sense if the theses under consideration were correct.

With respect to their agreement with the Magisterium of the Church, we refer to what is written in the text.[6]

6.   Law as a Structure of the Church

As we have said, the necessary nature of law in the people of God is based on the Church's structure. And indeed, law is not only an ordering of behavior but also a societal structure.

Frequently law has been defined generically as a *lex*, a rationale or a measurement of social life. But this truth must be interpreted more broadly than taking law as a rule of conduct, although in the last analysis, such regulation of conduct is the function of law, to which all other functions can be referred. A somewhat external view of the juridical phenomenon could lead to restricting law to the regulation of human conduct: follow such and such a procedure, perform these or other acts in this or that manner, etc. In that sense, law would be the norms that the subjects, judges, bishops or

---

6. Cf. D. CENALMOR and J. MIRAS, *El Derecho de la Iglesia*, 2nd ed., Pamplona, EUNSA, 2005, p. 45.

priests, for example, would have to follow in their activities; and there would be nothing more to the juridical world.

However, such a restricted view is not tenable. Certainly the norms that regulate a judges' activity—an apropos example—are law. But is being a judge anything other than a juridical situation? Is a judge not installed as a judge (not just regulated in his activities) by the law and does he not have powers that are juridical in nature? Another example might be the figure of the Roman Pontiff. Being the Pope involves charisms such as infallibility when teaching *ex cathedra*; but a member of the faithful cannot become Pope by receiving charisms. Charisms are received because of being the Pope. It is also true that being the Roman Pontiff implies the supernatural realities of being a bishop. But being the bishop of Rome is not the result of receiving a certain sacrament. Nor can a person be Pope because of receiving a special plenitude of episcopate, something like being a kind of super-bishop because of the bountiful effects of the sacrament received or of some special ontological supernatural realities. Being the Pope is a juridical situation created by divine law, with powers and faculties granted by divine law; a person has those powers because of legitimate accession to the Supreme Pontificate. And the Pope in the Church is its visible Head, who represents a bond of unity. As a last example, we can think of marriage. Being husband and wife, being married, is being united by a juridical bond which in no way excludes vital and ontological realities, for marriage is a function of those realities and assumes that they exist.

These examples could be multiplied *ad infinitum.* They show that law is not just a simple ordering of behavior. It is also a structure of societies and communities. It can even be one of their *constitutive* elements when the bonds that unite the members and make them into a cohesive unit are bonds of that nature. Law orders—it structures and organizes—a social group by creating bonds, establishing juridical situations, delimiting areas of jurisdiction and independence, granting powers and rights, etc. Canon law in relation to the people of God is no exception; law is a structure of the Church and not merely a norm for acting.

The structural function of law in the people of God has two modalities. In some cases it determines or completes the structure and organization of the Church by creating—legally, contractually, etc.—bonds, juridical situations or strictly juridical entities. These would run from figures of the Pope or the College of Bishops to figures of vicars general or judicial vicars, including religious or service contracts. Sometimes bonds or juridical situations include peculiar charisms (for example, the infallibility of the Pope, as mentioned above). They may be embodiments of a charism (for example, a foundational charism, in the case of religious), or they may even be the *res et sacramentum*, in the case of the sacrament of marriage.

Secondly, there are certain juridical structures with a different and broader dimension of structural and organizational factors; that dimension generally closes the cycle that makes up the structure. Being a Christian, for example, involves being a member of the people of God. But neither being a Christian nor being a member of the Church is solely or fundamentally a situation or bond of a juridical nature. Christians are united in an organization and consequently conform to a social structure through bonds of grace, through the action of the Holy Spirit and through the mystery of unity that is the Eucharist. Being a Christian is participating through Christ in the divine filiation. Being a member of the people of God is being united to it by all the mysterious bonds that make up the people of God. Analogously, being a priest or bishop is something more than holding a juridical position, because it is to have in the people of God a *sacerdotal* position that is much richer than just a juridical position. But being a Christian is *also* being juridically bound to the Church. A member of the faithful is not bound to the people of God and the hierarchy by mysterious bonds alone, but also by juridical bonds of solidarity and subjection. Likewise, being a priest involves a bond to the Church and to its hierarchy, with a duty to serve that is a juridical bond. In both cases, law completes the bonding by further determinations of a very different nature.

Together with ontological elements (ontological union), in the Church there is a juridical structure without which, given the current economy of salvation, something would be lacking in the constitution and organization of the Church as a society. This does not mean that only law exists in the Church. It also means that in the current economy of salvation, ecclesial ontological realities have a complementary juridical structure that completes the structuring and constitutive cycle of the people of God as convoked and founded by Christ. Although the bonds uniting members of the faithful in a common goal and the structure of the Church as a hierarchical society are supported by ontological realities tending to move toward solidarity among the faithful and toward making and using means of salvation, both bonding and hierarchical structure receive their fullness through the juridical structure.

That is the deep meaning of the juridical Church (*Ecclesia iuris*). This theological truth implies a greater penetration of law in the Church than the mere existence of a legislative power. In that sense, the juridical system is an organizing structure that, together with ontological elements, constitutes and organizes the people of God.

From such a point of view the basic factors in the juridical structure of the Church may be reduced to three: a) *constitutive factors*, among which are the bonds incorporating the faithful into the Church (the fundamental bond of being a member of the people of God), together with the bond to the hierarchy as a member of it, the creation of minor communities, etc.; b) *organizational factors* (ecclesiastical offices, for example); and c) *norms for evaluating and developing* the activities and behavior of the faithful and the hierarchy.

With that explanation we believe we have brought out the idea that law in the Church is not a superstructure, an extrinsic, added-on organization that favors the development of the people of God but remains a supplementary element. On the contrary, the Church is a juridical Church as well as a Church of charity (*Ecclesia caritatis*); one of its constituent factors is its juridical organization and structure.

Canon law must therefore be understood as the juridical structure of the Church. In that sense, canon law is a set of norms, but not only that; it is above all a system of juridical relationships, a complex of bonds that unites the faithful and *situates* them in a certain position (a juridical position) within the social body of the Church for the Church's ends. At the same time canon law includes that set of factors which creates the above-mentioned relationships, organizes the hierarchy or simply evaluates or regulates the behavior of the faithful.

APPENDIX

With respect to the law as a structure of the Church, we should make a terminological clarification, which can also be useful for all the rest of this first part. It has to do with the meaning used when we speak of law. As it is well known, the word *law* (*ius*) is used with different meanings, although all of them are related. As a follower of classical juridical realism, I understand that the law in its primary sense is what belongs to each one, because it is owed to him, according to the classical definition of justice: giving to each his own, his right. What is his, *suum*, becomes equivalent to *ius suum*; the right, what is just or *ipsa res iusta* in the words of Thomas Aquinas, is precisely what belongs to each one that, because it may or may not be in the hands of others, is owed him. This primary sense draws therefore analogical notions; it has an analogous principle: the juridical norm, which is the rule or statute of the law (*aliqua ratio iuris*, according to the Aquinate); the norm is called law in an analogous sense. Another analogical sense is also usually added: the subjective right.

At the same time, it is not uncommon, but rather customary, to speak of law in a very general sense, different from those seen thus far, albeit including them. Law is taken as a synonym of the *juridical phenomenon*, of the *juridical reality* to be more precise. This very general sense is what is used in the text.

The juridical reality or juridical phenomenon appears to us as a structure of the social reality, a complex structure that covers the *elements* and the *moments* of law. By elements, we understand those principles that we can call static: the subjects (with the subject of the personality), the bond that joins the subjects and the content of rights and obligations and other juridical situations that stem from the bond. These elements are organized in the *juridical relationship*, and all of them as a whole constitute the basis of the juridical system.

The moments of law are its dynamic principles, factors of organization and of change. The more significant are the norm (or the *lex* of the scholastics), private autonomy and judicial judgments, especially those creating precedents.

As it can easily be seen, the elements and moments of law are a structure, in this case a juridical structure.

It is in this very general and broad sense that we use the word law (*ius*) in the text.[7]

7.   *Sacramental Bases of Canon Law*

As we have just said, law is not a superstructure with respect to the supernatural roots of the people of God. We also spoke of the organizing function of the law. Taking a conciliar text as a basis, we also said that the people of God is "structured by the sacraments." Assuming that, we can then ask whether the law and the sacraments are related, or whether the structures born of the sacraments are different and diverge from the structures originating in the organizing

---

7. Cf. J. HERVADA, *¿Qué es el derecho? La moderna respuesta del realismo jurídico*, Pamplona, EUNSA, 2002, Santafé de Bogotá, ed. Colombiana, 2005; id., "Sugerencias acerca de los componentes del Derecho," *Ius Canonicum* VI (1966) 53–110.

force of the law. We must answer those questions by saying that canon law is based on the sacraments (in a special way on baptism and orders), and that the juridical system of the people of God in its primary nucleus is the juridical dimension of the *lex sacramentorum*, that is, the juridical dimension of the requirements, functions and norms of life that naturally spring from receiving the sacraments. A complete study of the subject would involve treating it especially in relation to baptism, confirmation, the Eucharist, orders and marriage. But to give an example of what we have just stated, we can refer briefly to baptism and orders, because they are the two sacraments of greatest importance with respect to canon law.

Baptism is the sacrament of becoming a member of the Church and it is the fundamental step in the personal process of salvation. Through baptism, a person is incorporated into Christ's body and with Christ shares the divine filiation, becoming a participant (*consors*) in the divine nature. By baptism a person also is incorporated into the Church as a full member, sharing all its benefits. As theologians say, the sacrament of baptism has a number of effects: sanctifying grace, character, etc. But of all its effects we are now particularly interested in the following: a) baptism incorporates a person fully into the Church; b) the baptized are destined for worship in the Christian religion (*LG* 11); c) the baptized person receives a calling to the apostolate and to participate actively in the life of the Church (*LG* 32 and 33; *AA* 3 and 10); and d) baptism requires living in accordance with Christ's teachings, which tends toward holiness.

All that we have been saying shows that a baptismal vocation has an inherent juridical expression: becoming a member of the Church involves a juridical bond. Baptism, with a unity of effects, makes a person a member of the people of God in all its complexity, including the juridical aspect, as the Church in its complex reality is one. A vocation for the apostolate, being destined for Christian worship, and the ability to participate actively in ecclesial life, assume that a Christian carries a juridical patrimony that consists of a set of rights and duties arising inherently (*iura nativa*) from having been baptized. In other words, the rights and duties are inherent in the efficacy of baptism, i.e., inherent in the participation in Christ which is the primordial effect of baptism. None of those juridical effects is an element superposed by a human legislator. Consequently, baptism does not act as a simple condition or requirement of a human norm that would give it juridical effect. As we have said, it is a juridical dimension inherent and innate in the radical condition of being baptized and participating in the dignity of the child of God just as natural rights are inherent in the dignity of a human being.

What are the consequences of what we have just stated? First, one of the fundamental nuclei of the Church's juridical structure as it now exists has its origin in the sacrament of baptism insofar as it generates new members of the Church and each day produces the bonds that continue to constitute the Church. Secondly, the set of human norms that governs the activities of the faithful and their position in the Church must be the realization and determination of the nucleus of juridical norms implied by the condition of a baptized person. In that sense, the norms of human law to which we have referred must tend toward developing the baptismal vocation, and that is the criterion of their justice and therefore of their juridical value. Thus human norms are not a superstructure but the cycle that completes the norms inherent in the condition of a baptized person. The rule that Saint Thomas established for human law if it conflicts with natural law would be applicable to any human norms that did not share those inherent characteristics: *non erit lex, sed legis corruptio.*

Similar reasoning can be used with respect to the sacrament of orders. This sacrament produces a unique and essentially different kind of participation in the priesthood of Christ. If all requisites are met, and that condition also applies to baptism, through the sacrament of orders, incorporation into the hierarchy is produced, a function within the people of God is received, and living in accordance with its own conditions is required. All those effects have a juridical dimension and all are the result of the efficacy of the sacrament. In the juridical sense and not only in the mysterious sense, the sacrament of orders is a *builder* of the Church, since it adds new members to the hierarchy. That, together with its structure and functions, fulfills a mission similar to the mission of baptism in its area by producing and making real the bonds that constitute the hierarchy. To summarize, the hierarchical structure of the people of God is made real through the sacrament of orders. The set of human norms that governs the activity of the hierarchy and its position within the Church should embody and determine the nucleus of juridical norms that include the condition of being ordained and receiving a mission.

An analysis of the other sacraments would lead us to similar conclusions, if we examined the nature and effects of each sacrament. The obvious conclusion is that there is harmony between juridical norms and the *lex sacramenti*, and also that the sacraments, especially baptism and orders, are factors that—on the existential level—make the Church real and structure it; and they also structure it juridically insofar as the sacraments produce juridical effects.

The nucleus of the sacraments as inherently juridical norms points to the relationship between divine law and human law. That is the subject we shall next study.

APPENDIX

Some years ago, I published an article titled *Las raíces sacramentales del derecho canónico* [The Sacramental Roots of Canon Law], which was subsequently translated into Italian and Portuguese.[8] If we compare this article and the

---

8. "Las raíces sacramentales del derecho canónico," in J. HERVADA, *Vetera et Nova*, 2nd ed., Pamplona, Navarra Gráfica Ediciones, 2005, pp. 297–319; "Le radici sacramentali del diritto canonico," *Ius Ecclesiæ* XVII [2005] 629–658. The Portuguese translation appeared in *Theologica* XVIII [1983], fasc. I–IV.

corresponding section of this book, we can note a fundamental coincidence: canon law sinks its roots in the sacraments, in the *lex sacramentorum*, using *lex* in the broad
meaning of the economics of salvation.

However, I would like to point out the differences
between both texts, which are not substantial in content, but
in perspective. In the aforementioned article, I discussed the
sacraments as *res iustæ*, as salvific goods that belong to them,
that belong to the faithful by virtue of their participation in
the merits of Christ, because they are *alter Christus, ipse
Christus*. It is the vision of classical juridical realism.

On the other hand, in this book, what I am trying to do is
highlighting the *juridical efficacy* of the sacraments, their
juridical effects as *builders* of the Church, that is, as causes of
the fundamental juridical relationships of the People of God.

In both cases, I reach the same conclusion: canon law is
based on and has its roots in the sacraments.[9]

8.   Divine Law and Human Law

Law is an order that does not arise solely from a human
legislator. Specifically and with reference to the Church, the
people of God recognize that there is a divine order within
them that is the base and foundation of their whole organization. Furthermore, the ecclesiastical legislator expresses
himself in a manner that is radically dependent upon divine
law, also called *Christ's law*, and there are a number of historical examples that could be cited. The history of the Church,
together with the human failures that may have occurred in
practice gives constant witness to that fundamental idea.
This dependence has been defended at the cost of persecu-
tions, schisms and heresies, and reflected in the "non
possumus" that has frequently echoed through the centuries
when attempts have been made to deviate from that law.

---

9. Cf. D. CENALMOR and J. MIRAS, *op. cit.*, note 6, pp. 45–51.

This order, called *divine law* by doctrine insofar as it represents a just social order, can be considered to be made up of the following factors: a) Foundational norms, given by Christ, which are collected in the New Testament or have been transmitted by tradition and which trace basic traits of the organization of the Church and fundamental guidelines for the social life of the people of God; for example, the primacy of Peter. b) Principles and requirements of the *lex sacramentorum* and in general of the *lex gratiæ*, which emanate from the order rooted in supernatural realities. These principles and requirements are distinguished from those in the preceding group, although it is not always easy to do so. The phenomenon is analogous to that of the natural law with regard to human nature; i.e., a system of norms rooted in supernatural realities. c) The principles and requirements of natural law that are also valid in the Church; they are integrated into the order of salvation but they are fully respected.

All of the above assumes that there are the following: a) social structures (relationships, bonds, rights and duties, hierarchical bodies, etc.) established by Christ and that actually exist once the acts or facts which, by virtue of Christ's will are their causes, are carried out; b) certain principles and requirements that human law must respect and consider as a point of departure because it is heavily dependent upon them.

An excessively literal application of a normativistic conception of canon law (which has been justly criticized) causes some theologians to show divine law in a rather curious manner and make the notion incomprehensible to anyone with a minimum of ecclesiological sensitivity. It appears as if divine law were a kind of code of stereotypical precepts that could be drawn up by condensing Scriptural texts and statements of the Tradition particularized in light of the Magisterium. That would give us a totally insufficient, rigid and static view of divine law. The term *divine law* signifies those aspects of Christ's founding will and divine design for the Church with consequences that can be related to what in the language of human culture we call law. In that sense divine law is in the word of God, which lives on in the Church. Revelation—insofar as it shows us a community congregated to hear the Word, celebrating the Eucharist and the other sacraments, and continuously inspired by grace— indicates the fundamental lines of ecclesial order, which is the harmony between pastoral action and liberty, obedience and autonomy. Thus, through revelation, the life of the Church calls for a consistency between law and the fullness of the Word as manifested in sacramental ontology; and also calls for a consistency between law and charismatic action. It is coherence that impels the faithful and enables them to act lawfully in the service of the community.

The divine order, however, is not the complete structure, organization and ordering of the life of the Church. Beside it there is human law which is not only an additional or supple- mentary order, because relative to the divine one it has char- acteristic functions that are due to the participation granted to the human being in the course of the history of salvation.

First, the norms given by Christ draw only the grand lines of the Church's organization and the fundamental require- ments of Christian life that are constantly being enriched through history as they meet with new realities. Second, the principles of divine law by definition do not imply a complete order because they are only principles; that order should there- fore be completed by human regulatory acts.

At the same time, other facts must be kept in mind. The ecclesiastical Magisterium has the mission of clarifying, fixing and interpreting the existence, scope and content of divine law so that it may be observed. In addition, knowl- edge of divine law is not automatically thorough from the beginning; its contents are continually being discovered as the faithful's awareness delves deeper into the complex meaning and depth of the Christian message and at the same time as its requirements are understood when meeting new situations. Last, regardless of recognizing the validity and imperative nature of divine law, we can scientifically wonder if the specific nature of divine law is truly juridical or are they norms of a different type. That all raises a number of questions that for our purpose may be condensed into three: a) the nature of divine law; b) the relationship between divine law and human law; and c) the need and means for positivizing divine law.

a)   The Nature of Divine Law

The explicit or implicit answer given by contemporary canonical doctrine to the question of the nature of divine law has not been unanimous. Following a long doctrinal tradition, most authors feel that both divine law and human law are properly and truly law. They are two types of juridical norms that flow together to govern the Church and are distinguished by their source or origin. Other authors maintain that only human law fits the concept of law and, therefore, divine law, the obligatory nature of which they do not question, has a different nature. Some of those authors ignore the question of the nature of divine norms (Del Giudice, for example). Others have held that divine norms are moral norms in matters of justice (Van Hove, Naurois), or theological—juridical rules (d'Avack), or they feel that they represent ethical requirements (Di Robilant with respect to natural law), or orders of justice with a similar nature to human law (Pérez Mier).

We believe that before we can give an answer to the question of the nature of divine law, two things must be considered. First, things are often described as divine, natural, or positive law, when, regardless of their nature, they are not. Law, imperative norms and binding structures, cannot be confused with its determining factors. Neither the nature of things (the nature of a person is another matter), nor the norms of common sense or prudence are norms of divine law; these are either physical factors or rational factors, but they cannot be considered to be true juridical norms merely by themselves. Divine law also cannot be confused with the rules of experience, the dictates of juridical awareness or doctrinal truths, no matter how universally accepted, so long as they involve only juridical *wisdom* and not an imperative social order. A truth or a wise norm is not the same as the law. In that sense, and as we have said, there are many rules or factors confused with natural or divine— positive law, without being law. True divine law is composed only of a just social order that is imperative and binding; it arises from the legislative will of God, and in the Church, by the founding will of Christ.

In the second place, now within the nucleus of norms that we call divine law, we must distinguish the elements to which we have previously referred: *norms*, given by Christ, which order and value behavior, or establish bonds and situations within the people of God. There are *principles of order and requirements of justice that are inherent* in a Christian person and in the nature of the Church. They may be immutable or they may be relative to the Church's history and the constant emergence, transformation, or disappearance of various situations.

If we look at the problem this way, there is no doubt— nor does doctrine any longer doubt—that the first group of elements of divine law is what is properly and truly law. It is an order with all the facets that belong to the notion of law: social, just, imperative, intersubjective and historical (i.e., currently in force in history). Relative to this last facet, we would like to add a few words. These norms were historically dictated by Christ, an actual man, with powers as such, although by virtue of the hypostatic union. And these norms are in force in human history because of the binding force of Christ's will, for, through the sacraments and the Church itself as the sacrament of salvation, the divine elements that constitute those norms are present and stay in history with all their original force.

As for the second group of the elements of divine law, they are also law; that is, they have a juridical nature but act as what they are: principles and requirements. In human law there are also such principles. They are either established in declarations considered to be fundamental laws or inherent in an organized State in accordance with political doctrine, ideologies or governing mentalities. They are collected as juridical principles or recognized as requirements of the current juridical order. Those principles and requirements act as informational factors and as limitations on the use of power; power can do nothing against them, from issuing laws to issuing administrative acts. But since they are not complete norms and because they are consequently general rather than specific, they do not acquire full regulatory efficacy until they are completed by legislative activity. Similarly, the principles and requirements of divine law in the Church act as *shaping factors*, as *limits* on the activity of the ecclesiastic hierarchy and as a *necessary basis* for human law; but they cannot have a greater juridical effect until they are developed into real norms because they are general and non-specific. In addition, it is advisable to note that many of those principles and requirements are not expressed by one possibility alone, but by several; thus for them to be fully effective, the legislator must opt or choose among them.

b) The Relationship Between Divine Law and Human Law

There has also not been complete agreement in doctrine concerning the relationship between divine law and human law. For the majority, divine law is the foundation of human law; divine law prevails over human law and converges with it in governing the life of the Church. Since divine law is the foundation of human law, the content of human law is determined by and is the conclusion drawn from norms or principles of a divine order. Human power receives its authority from divine law. Bellini, for his part, has described human law as an autonomous system of law but materially and formally subordinated to divine law. Bellini holds this opinion in contrast to other authors who, whether or not they deny the juridical nature of divine law, understand human law to be constructed as a primary system of law. They consider it to be *original* (the *juridical* effect of its norms does not derive from any other system of law, not even the divine order), and *self-sufficient* (any situation or social relationships will find an applicable norm in the human system without having recourse to the divine order as such).

Divine law and human law together form a single juridical system. The principle of unity between divine and human law is threefold. First, the Church's basic juridical structure (juridical bonds among the faithful, the hierarchical organization of divine law) exists because of divine law. All other structures are derivative, complementary or historical forms developed from that basic structure. At all times in history, all other structures are integrated into the Church's basic juridical structure and together with it they form the complete structure of the people of God. Second, people have authority and that authority is one source of law, by virtue of divine law. Human authority is not original per se and does not receive its strength from the members of the Church. Lastly, all social realities within the Church, even if only inchoatively, have their own embryonic order (the law of nature in some cases, the law of grace for the rest). From that order, the human legislator, by the method of determination or of conclusion (*S. Th.*, I–II, q. 95, yr. 3), deduces a positive norm. Under these three principles, divine law and human law form a single juridical system of law.

Together with their unity, the two types of law have a hierarchical relationship. Divine law is the *fundamental law*, the *necessary basis* and the *limits* of human law. That is why human norms that conflict with divine law are disaffirmed by divine norms (true *higher canonical authorities*, in the words of Journet). Because they are of a superior rank, divine norms can cause the invalidity of human norms in some cases, and can always make them illicit; but human norms can be reformed or adapted if, without conflicting with divine law, they prove to be inadequate to it.

c)   The Positivization and Formalization of Divine Law

The problem of the positivization of divine law has been raised only by authors who either deny the juridical nature of divine law or who hold that divine and human law are two separate systems of law. Those doctrinal stances do agree, although with some strong differences, that a divine norm is not transformed into a juridical norm in the canonical system unless it is *formally accepted* by positive human law. By the act of acceptance—*canonizatio,* according to an expression coined by Del Giudice—divine norms are transformed into law and specifically, into canon law.

Having said these things, it is superfluous to add that we do not think that this theory of positivization seems right. Divine law in the Church is not a different system of law from human law. Both divine and human laws are a single juridical order. Divine law needs no approval or acceptance by ecclesiastical powers to be the law that is in effect. Rather, the opposite is true, as Bellini says; human law is objectively subordinate, both materially and formally, to divine law. This does not mean that the need to positivize divine law should be rejected out of hand. On the contrary, it seems that properly taken, positivization is true to the very nature of law because law is essentially a historical system; it is a historical and temporal dimension of human reality, and at the same time evolving. This raises a question. Only an imperative system that goes back to a historical factor in its force and immediate source can be considered to be law. Otherwise, as in the case of *lex æterna,* it cannot be called law even if it is obligatory and binding. Therefore, divine norms cannot be called law if they cannot be traced back to a historical factor. Catholic theology has overcome that difficulty in the case of natural law. It states that natural law is *promulgated* (the passage to historical efficacy) in human nature itself in the form of first principles of practical reason and as a person's requirements. In the case of divine *positive* law, the passage toward being historical was made by Revelation, which is a truly historical event, and by the existence of those realities of which positive divine law is its juridical dimension. All that is true, but it is not the complete answer. To see the subject in all its complexity it must be studied first in relation to a) the effective operating capacity of the norm; then b) the perfecting and integrating function of human law; and finally c) the types or forms of positivization of the law.

a) Whether divine or human, a juridical norm is a ruling act or mandate from the very moment it is promulgated. After promulgation, it is in force and is binding upon its subjects. But a subject is a free being and may refuse to comply with the law. If a person does not obey, the norm loses none of its force, but it has no practical force. Similarly, a member of society has an imperative order that arises from the requirements of the person's dignity (the law of nature or natural law). However, society may impose on itself a system of *laws* that are accepted as effectively functioning and valid but that are not in harmony with the natural order. In this case too, natural law is still binding and obligatory, but it is de facto ineffective. Society as such is governed by a system of norms that, even though they are contrary to divine law, are accepted and obeyed as laws governing the social relations of the members of society. In this case, divine law will in fact be outside of the *legal* system that actually governs society. In that sense, there can be no doubt that divine law by itself is effective in the life of a society if it has been accepted by the society. However, it is one thing that acceptance by society produces effective operability of the divine norms in social relationships, and a very different thing that causes them to be binding.

But such a problem cannot properly be raised in canon law. The Church is not merely a human society but an institution, the people of God, founded by Christ, who is both God and Man. It is also the Mystical Body of Christ which receives a continual and vital inflow from its Head. The will of the Church, *qua* social body considered institutionally, identifies itself with the Divine will, and it accomplishes this through a union of its own will with that of God (hence her theological claim to be the *Bride of Christ*). The Church is so by virtue of constitutional law—against which the will of those who are baptized has no powers—and it is so by virtue of the supernatural and charismatic realities of its very being. The people of God that continue Christ's mission are constitutionally and objectively ordered for the purpose of establishing the divine order in all aspects of human life. Thus all of divine law is received into the Church constitutionally and completely. It is true that human powers, because they are not infallible, can issue erroneous norms and even positively unjust norms. But as we were saying, such laws are invalidated by higher canonical instances.

There is, however, one fact that qualifies what we have just said. The constitutional reception of divine law means what we might call "the constitutional will to comply with it"; but that does not mean that divine law is totally and fully known. The same happens here as with the truths of faith. From the beginning the Church has totally accepted revealed truth; but that does not mean that there are some truths that are unknown at any given moment in history or only imperfectly understood. However, the entire deposit of faith, whether known or unknown, is radically accepted. Likewise, certain norms of divine law may be imperfectly understood or even unknown, and consequently may not be followed or are imperfectly followed. But this is always a process of *learning* or *experience* and it is not inconsistent with a radical and constitutional acceptance of these norms. Even so, this becoming aware by the Church is a phase in the passage to the historical existence of the divine norms, at least with respect to the fullness of the passage to the historical efficacy as law.

It is in this sense that divine law needs to be *positivized*. By that we must understand not its radical acceptance within canon law by an act of human authority, nor its transformation into law, but its passage to coming into force in history by an ecclesial awareness of its specific content. Thus a simply magisterial statement or universal reception by the *sensus fidei*—as a point of faith—is sufficient for an unknown or disputed norm in divine law to have an immediate historical efficacy; it must then be accepted by the faithful and by the hierarchy as a juridical norm. For a little-known divine norm, a magisterial statement sets the content depending upon the degree of knowledge reached at any moment in history and makes present the "constitutional will to obey it." But it does not presuppose nor require an act of reception *ex novo* by the authorities.

To understand the precise limits of the idea of positivization, we need to spend some time on clarifications. A juridical order that has already been formed is not merely a confused and scattered set of norms of equal value. The system has guiding and informing principles, different types of norms with different force, different mechanisms for applying the laws, different embodiments of each of the acts concerned, and different requirements needed for each of the factors in the system to be valid or for giving each a certain value, and so forth. This is a technically structured order that conditions and, through its technical mechanisms, shapes the force and application of the law. In sum, a juridical system that has already been formed is a *formalized* system. What does *formalization* mean? It consists of giving a technical character to the different factors and elements which make up the law by means of the granting of a particular form, the attribution of a precise efficiency, in themselves and with regard to others, the supplying of technical instruments for the fulfillment and the guarantee of its efficiency, the establishment of conditions and requisites in order for these elements and factors to be valid or efficient, etc. Through this there is a tendency toward fully seeing to the guarantee of the function and value of each juridical element or factor within the context of a concrete system of law.

In the face of this reality which originates by virtue of the need for certainty, security, and justice in the juridical order, positivization must be completed by formalization. For this reason, divine law once positivized must be integrated by means of formalization through ecclesiastical norms which complete it or which establish the mechanisms that guarantee its applications, etc. Thus, for example, the *ius conubii* (the right to marriage)—a natural right—is formalized within the canonical system of law through the establishment of its limits (capacity), requisites for its exercise, the form of the celebration of marriage and the correspondent registry attesting to its existence, nullity or separation procedures, etc. Without this opportune formalization, divine law would only imperfectly be integrated within the canonical system of law since it would be pending upon good will and a correct sense of justice on the part of those who must fulfill it and apply it for social effectiveness. By integrating divine law within the whole of the mechanisms granting it a technical character formalization places at its disposal all the resources it needs in order to be applied correctly.

From what has been said, it follows that non-positive divine law must not be confused with non-formalized divine law. Furthermore, it is possible to come across a pre-formalized divine law, that is, divine law which is lacking the adequate and desired formalization.

b) Having examined the first point, we may now pass on to the second. There are two other types of norms or principles within divine law, together with a primary nucleus of norms that completely govern a social relationship:

- norms that indicate a generic juridical relationship, that are made concrete by human norms;

- principles and requirements inherent in the realities of Church history, in its developmental sphere and in the advent of new structures. In these new situations there is also a nucleus of divine order (natural law or the law of grace) that human law must respect (principles and requirements). In all those cases there is one constant: an order that needs to be completed by human law. That is especially true for the second case where, rather than an incomplete order, there is the first instance of an order.

Evidently in both of the above cases, the legislator's function is properly authoritative:

- because it completes the natural or supernatural order with a positive law, without which social relations could not be fully regulated due to their indeterminateness;

- because—and this is valid only for a new or changed situation—the hierarchy has the mission of governing and regulating social life, and consequently of recognizing or not any new situations of human origin, always in accordance with justice. These have a human origin because they are historical developments driven by human actions, although they may obey an influence from the Holy Spirit. Under that principle, the order initiated in these situations is a requirement of justice that binds the legislator at the time of regulating new situations, but it is not perfected in its nature in the juridical order except by recognizing the newly created situation. Before there is recognition, we can speak of the demands of justice, but not of fully developed norms. In those cases, positivization is required and is authoritative. But positivization *perfects* (completes the order) and *integrates* (the divine requirements or principles become integrated within the completed human norm), so that the nucleus of divine law that may exist possesses the proper force of such law (*St. Th.*, I–II, q. 95, a. 2).

c) Finally, we shall make a few brief comments on the methods of positivizing divine law. Positivization produced in the process of integrating divine law into human law is related to the sources of human positive law. These are principally law and custom, but also the integrating function of a judge in specific cases, and doctrine under c. 19 of the *CIC*. But positivization understood as discovery and awareness of divine law takes place in different ways in the Church, as we have repeatedly pointed out: the ecclesiastical Magisterium, canonical and theological doctrine, the sense of faith and even the social dynamism of Christian life lived and proclaimed according to convictions born of having true charisms or a sense of faith.

In this regard we must point out the close connection between faith and ecclesial life. Catholic faith is essentially dynamic; it operates as the root and source of Christian life, which finds its dynamic strength, its value and justification in faith. Therefore a norm that is believed through faith is *necessarily* an operative law. A norm taught and believed by the Church is for the Church (for the social body considered as such and for its members) a norm for acting and living. A norm that was taught and not embodied in legislation would be a *scandal*—a contradiction between faith and works; it would not accord with the essential nature of the Church as the sacrament of salvation. It would be a clear case of human law that was not law but a corruption of law (tyranny). And that is because faith is a norm of acting. Thus the discovery of a truth that involves a norm of acting (divine law) is a positivization of divine law by the very force of faith and the constitution of the Church. In the Church there can be no break between faith and the Church's juridical order. Such a break is condemned from the start to have no juridical force by the Church's constitutional and foundational norms that receive, once and forever, all of divine law.

APPENDIX

Also, in recent years, certain writers—not many, but very active writers—have tried to create a "crisis of divine law," have made problematic its very nature as law. Let us consider an assertion published in the aforementioned year 2004:

> C'è dunque, un forte problema terminologico: lo *jus divinum* è chiamato "Diritto" (*nomen habet*) ma non lo è (*non est*)! Esso infatti non ricade sotto nessuna delle specifiche d'individuazione del Diritto come tale. Ciò non significa escludere l'esistenza di una "regolamentazione comportamentale normative" di origine divina, tanto a livello di Creazione [no doubt the author is alluding to natural law] che di Rivelazione [positive

divine law], ma semplicemente se ne riconose la non-giuridicità teorica (né ontologica), in quanto mancano le caratteristiche individuative essenziali del Diritto: ogget-tività, separabilità, coercibilità, all'interno di un gruppo sociale istituzionalizzato.

Nevertheless, in the same paragraph cited above, we can see where the sophism lies. He says "all'interno di un gruppo sociale *istituzionalizzato*." For that writer, there is no law other than within an institutionalized group; however, he is one of those who defend the shift from the charism to the operative institution, according to proponents of this thesis, in the Church. Since institutionalization would be a human process, there would only be positive human law within it, divine law vanishes, would not have a place in the Church. But we have already noticed that those theses of institutionalization are not adequate and, moreover, are not in agreement with the Catholic doctrine on the Church. Therefore, the denial of the *ius divinum* that is declared in that paragraph—and that the author develops much more—is a fallacy. The *ius divinum* not only has the *nomen iuris*, but also has it because *ius est*.

That type of "vanishing" of divine law comes, at times, through another channel: it is stated as law, which it is not, and in this way divine law disappears as law. Let us consider the following claim: "Parola e Sacramento sono realtà di natura giuridica per il fatto che si pongono tra due soggetti (Dio e l'uomo) e creano una situazione di doverosità (la risposta dell'uomo a Dio) carica di conseguenze (l'otteni-mento della salvezza)." Obviously, this is from a follower of the Munich School, which bases canon law in the Word and the sacraments. But in this case, the argument is unfounded, because the relationship to which it refers does not have a juridical nature, it is not law; the author is confused in attrib-uting to it "natura giuridica." In any event, the consequence with respect to the *ius divinum* is clear: it is not real law.

In fact, according to the claim in this phrase, one cannot deduce that the Word and the sacraments are of a juridical nature, because the relations between God and man are not law. This is a bit elementary; the relation between God and man is characterized by the disparity between the divine benefits and man's capacity to compensate for them, man is incapable of paying the debt; on the other hand, what is characteristic of law is the proportion or equality between the good owed and the payment of the debt. Even if those relations contain a duty (which they do) and in them man brings to bear his salvation, the God—man relations are in no way juridical relations: they are relations of another kind, which traditionally have been called moral—if they refer to norms—or, from another more intense and complete perspective, of *religion* or *religation*. Precisely the distinction between moral and law—in their aspect as norm—has been made in the fact that the moral norm regulates man's relations with God, while law is characteristic of the relations between men: *inter homines* and also *inter gentes* (according to the phrasing of Vitoria, Suárez, and subsequent writers).

What is most needed now is to make it clear that law, any law, including canon law, is a *human order.* In its primary sense, law is what is just or owed with a debt in the strict sense, of justice, between men; only between them are there relations of a juridical nature. In an analogical sense, law is manifested in the norm or *law,* and it is the statute of law (*aliqua ratio iuris* according to the well-known formula of Thomas Aquinas), the regulating rule of human relations, of the community or human *societas,* according to justice. Only between men is there a juridical norm.

That is why what is claimed in some recent canonical writings cannot be accepted: the Alliance between God and the People chosen through the Law of Moses would be a juridical pact, because it is made with a people or community, unlike the promises and alliances of Yahweh with Noah, Abraham and other patriarchs, which would be pacts with individual persons.

Naturally, the Alliance of God with the chosen People is a pact that, in that it is between God and men, does not belong to law; it is not an Alliance or promise of a juridical nature. I stress that it belongs to the relations of religation of man with God, to *religion*, of a sacred nature that is much superior to law. Certainly the Law of Moses contains juridical precepts (it is something that is well-known and does not need to be stressed), but those juridical precepts—what are called by medieval theologians *præcepta iudicialia*—are those norms that regulate what is just or the relations of justice between the members of the Old People of God, that is, the social life of Israel.

In short, law is a human order, *inter homines* and *inter gentes*. And it is a reality *huius sæculi*, without eschatological transcendence.

Some canonists of the latest generation, based on the fact that law is a human order, change this idea to maintain that, in that it is a human order, there is only positive law or *ius humanum*, consequently denying the fact that divine law is law; they consider it to be theology, the bases of canon law (understood as positive law), etc.

They are writers who, with different nuances, understand that divine law—natural and positive according to some, others omit natural law and set their attention on positive divine law only—transcends history and that it is "historified"—that is the word they usually use—, it passes to history, in positive human law. That is why, in human history, in the *sæculum*, according to an ancient form of speaking, or *in hoc sæculo*, according to a more modern use, but the three expressions having the same meaning, in human history, I repeat, only positive law or positive human law would exist. This positive law is contingent, and therefore it does not possess *necessary*—theological—elements, that is, elements of divine law. Hence the pastoralist orientation speaks of the *destheologization* of canon law, reducing it to something malleable, applicable according to pastoral needs, although there is no shortage of those who claim that if the pastoral occasion postulates it, it must be applied *contra litteram* of the written norm.

The key point, as we can see, is "historification," although it has already been said that among the various authors there is a variety of nuances. They also agree that positive law is contingent, that is, it lacks the necessary elements internal to it.

More specifically, for example, there is no shortage of writers who distinguish between the essence of the Church as a dogmatic reality and the historical form of its existence, as a contingent reality, so that divine law would belong to the essence of the Church, while positive ecclesial law would affect the contingent institutional reality thereof. Logically divine law disappears from human history, from the *sæculum*. In it there is a clear separation between the essence and the historical existence of the Church.

However, there is something inconsistent in this, if we assume that the author is using the terms in a common scientific sense, because otherwise he should have noted it and indicated the new meaning of those words. What is essence? Essence is a metaphysical concept that expresses that whereby a being is what it is and not anything else. And it is a *being of reason with a foundation* in re *or in reality*. This essence is *realized*, becomes real, in the existing entity of which it is a metaphysical component, and we call it *nature* because it is a principle of operation. No existing being—not the Church either—can lack a nature and, therefore, an essence; it is impossible. Instead of existence, it would be more accurate to speak of *actus essendi*, but in order to put us at the level of the thesis we are analyzing, there does not appear to be any problem in speaking of existence or *history*. In this sense, "historification" is nothing more than the shift from mental reality—supremely in God—to existence, to the real being existing through the *actus essendi*, that is, the shift to history.

Given this, it is obvious that what distinguishes between an essence as a dogmatic reality and a contingent historical form, is not possible, because in the existing real, *historical*, being of the Church, the essence as dogmatic reality must necessarily be *realized*, made real, therefore in no way is the historical form of the Church contingent. It is known to have contingent aspects, but it is not totally contingent, because in its existing historical reality it has a *dogmatic* dimension—to use the author's terminology—and within it the *ius divinum* as truly existing and valid law, because it is one of the aspects which the author calls the dogmatic reality of the Church. The conclusion is that the thesis in question is unfounded.

Equally unfounded is this author's opinion regarding natural law and natural right, which also "vanishes."

Setting aside some secondary aspects that do not affect the core of his thesis, such as asserting that natural law cannot be followed (cannot be complied with) without grace, which is a half-truth, I will concentrate on the fundamentals.

According to this writer, natural law, written in the heart of man (Rom. 2:15), is contained in the nature of man and can be known through reason with regard to participation in the eternal law. However, natural law, because it is inscribed in nature, "trascende la *storia*," it *transcends* history, but at the same time it is historically known and performed by man. So then natural law is "historified" by being known and performed. He confirms this thesis of the "historification" of natural law further on. Natural law and natural right express, as ontological realities, the dignity of the human person by determining the natural rights and duties and, on the basis of the self-understanding that man has, become "historified" in positive law and in positive right. That is, they are "historified" through man's self-understanding.

The mistake here is obviously that he considers that natural law transcends history, because it is in inscribed in nature—which is inaccurate, because the place it is inscribed is in natural practical reason through sinderesis. Natural reason is a power of the human person—which is fully history—perfected, with respect to natural law, through the innate virtue of sinderesis. Therefore, it is totally history. What transcends human history is the eternal law, and this law, which is identified with the divine essence, is the law that passes to human history, is "historified," in natural law, which, because it is inscribed in the natural reason of each historically existing human person—as the patrimony of his rational being—does not need any historification but is fully history. Saying that natural law or natural rights are "historified" through the work of man through his self-understanding and his actions has no basis, and concluding from it that natural law—divine law—"vanishes," and all that is left is positive (human) law is in no way acceptable.

Now that we have seen natural divine law, let us consider positive divine law. And because we are discussing canon law, we should focus on the *evangelical law* or law of Christ. To be more precise, what concerns us is the law that represents the juridical dimension of the foundational will of Christ.

In this assumption, various writers coincide in the same opinion with differing nuances: divine law either does not exist as law or it transcends history, whereby it is "historified" in positive (human) law, which is contingent, without theological factors or other *necessary* elements. The key point in all of them is what they call "historification," the passage to human history, to the *sæculum* of the ancients. Perhaps the clearest position is that of those authors which we already discussed who maintain that in the primitive Church, the shift from the charism and the charismatic leaders to institutionalization was brought about by human actions; in this case, the foundational Will of Christ adopts juridical factors, not in itself, but through "historification" through human action by means of positive (human) law.

In all the variations and nuances of these theories contrary to the *ius divinum*, we find a faulty understanding of the mystery of the Incarnation of the Word. The Word incarnate, *perfectus Deus et perfectus homo* (Athanasian Symbol), by virtue of the assumed human nature and as (divine) *person*, it is immersed in human history. As Saint John writes: "Et Verbum caro factum est, et *habitavit in nobis*." Christ is not outside of human history, of the *sæculum*, but immersed in it. The Athanasian symbol also says it: "Deus est ex substantia Patris ante sæcula genitus: et homo est *ex substantia matris in sæculo natus*." Born of a woman in history, *in sæculo*, Christ has a genealogy, is a descendant of Abraham, Isaac, Jacob, and Judas, and above all is a descendant of David, his offspring, in which the Davidic promises are fulfilled: "the Lord God will give him the throne of David, his father, he will reign eternally over the house of Jacob, and his Kingdom will be without end." David is called by the archangel Gabriel the *father*, ascendant, of Jesus. He is a member of the People of Israel through circumcision, from a nuclear family (Saint Joseph, Saint Mary, and Him) and from an extended family, his clan, his "brothers," etc. Christ is a historical figure, *in sæculo natus*, without needing anything for his full insertion into history, for his "historification."

There is nothing lacking *in his acts and in his words*, to be fully and totally immersed *in hoc sæculo*, in human history. This is the Catholic faith regarding the Incarnation of the Word.

Therefore, what Christ established in the Church with a juridical dimension—for example, the Primacy of Peter, the Apostolic College, the sacraments, rules of conduct, etc.—is fully historical. That divine law does not transcend history, the *sæculum*, nor does it need any "historification" factor. Speaking of the need or the fact of a subsequent "historification" of human origin has no valid basis. That is why that thesis of the "historification" of divine law (which would transcend human history or would not be in it) through a human action constituting positive (human) law, is not only a juridical error, but also a Christological error. In short, divine—natural and positive—law is true valid law.[10]

---

10. Taken from: J. ESCRIVÁ, *Relectura de la obra científica de Javier Hervada*, being prepared.

II. THE SCIENCE OF CANON LAW

A. *Juridical Knowledge*

1. *Preliminary Considerations*

Law is a dimension of social reality that gives it order. Law is the rationale or measure of social life, presided over by the principle of justice. Law is in part a given order (natural and divine—positive law), and in part man's creation. It always requires a moment in time when it is put into practice—living in accordance with the law, which is living in accordance with justice.

In order to be created, law needs to be legislated in accordance with its nature; to be lived, it needs to be known. In both cases, although with differences, it is necessary to have *criteria*, a working *method* and a certain amount of *knowledge*. The same occurs in the other facets of the life of human beings; to obtain something, to perform an act properly, it is not enough to want to do it, it is necessary to know how to do it.

Being a jurist or, in general, living according to law is *knowing how* to do so. It assumes a specific intellectual habit (dianoetic) that consists in knowing how to make a just social order within Society. Similarly, being a canonist is having an intellectual habit directed toward establishing a just social order within the Christian community. Finally, being a canonist consists in being a technician in justice, which is a necessary dimension of the people of God.

2.   Knowledge and Juridical Reality

Law and science are not and cannot be confused. Law is a reality that exists outside the mind; it is an objective order belonging to intelligent beings, and it is more than just a simple idea. But the fact that there is an order of intelligent beings emphasizes the necessity of the participation of the human mind so that this order may exist. What is the role of this participation of intelligence? Is it pure knowledge, or is it also an operation that produces, or to put it more exactly, constructs the law?

As we were saying, the law is both a given reality, an object of knowing, and an operable reality that can be constructed, an object of action. Indeed, if we look at law in relation to its legislative phase, no one can doubt that the law is something drawn up by human beings. Laws are social regulations that humans establish according to criteria of various types (technical, juridical, political, for civil society, or pastoral, for canon law, etc.). But social reality is not itself a subject without being normative. In society there is an innate order, or also, in the case of the law of the Church, an order established by Christ. These are sectors of juridical reality that the human person knows, but does not create. In that case, reality is something that can be known.

In addition, from the point of view of applying and complying with the law, it must be known to be lived. There is, then, an indubitable cognitive dimension in this way of looking at it. Moreover, for law to be lived it must be *concretized*. What do we mean by concretized? Jurists usually also say it must be complied with, or more precisely, *applied*. A norm or a duty exists from the time it formally takes effect. Norms and duties are, nevertheless, categories that must be realized by being applied to the social reality that they are designed to shape. The process of applying the law is precisely one aspect of constructing the law in its primary sense; it is the reality justly organized, as it is understood by the doctrine of juridical realism. Consequently, living the law (in its normative sense or sense as a juridical structure) is, at the right time, a process of constructing juridical reality, a product of *knowing how,* as we previously mentioned.

3. Science and Decision

Knowing is proper to *science;* operating or constructing requires *art* (according to the ancient classic term) or *technique* (in modern terminology). Thus, we need to distinguish the science of law in a general sense from the technique or art of law.

Theoretically and generally speaking, the concepts of science and technique or art are different. For example, there is a science of speculative knowledge of painting. A connoisseur of painting *knows* about artists, paintings, the different schools of painting and can even be a critic or make appraisals. Along with the science, there are various degrees of the art or technique of painting. Those who possess it are called artists, experts, etc., depending upon the degree and type of art or technique that they possess. They are the ones with the *skill* to paint a picture, reproduce it or restore it. This skill or talent is not called science, but art or technique.

However, the science and technique of law are not separate concepts. On the contrary, the so-called technique of law is integrated into science as one of its instrumental factors. This is so because juridical science is not a speculative science, but a practical science.

The purpose of speculative science is simply to learn about an object, and its work terminates with the knowledge obtained. Whether the object is in itself something given or whether it is also something that can be put into practice is irrelevant because in either case speculative science tends only to learn about it.

On the other hand, the purpose of practical science is to do something, something which is formally considered as such, that is, the purpose of operation. A practical science is knowledge intentionally directed to achieving the purpose.

It therefore follows that in a practical science, the idea of doing something specific governs the method and the specific of investigation.

But making law at the time of producing it, applying it, is not purely knowledge nor just having a skill. It requires a *decision* to be made in which the will p lays an important role. The decision is the product of juridical prudence. The science of law is directed toward this kind of decision and enriches the cognoscitive dimension (it does not suffice to want something; as we said earlier, it is necessary to know how to do it). In addition, in the final analysis, the aforementioned technical factors come together to make a decision possible. Thus there is between juridical science and juridical prudence a connection that integrates them into an intentional unit.

Next we shall analyze the subject from a panoramic viewpoint. We shall present an overall view of juridical knowledge, together with more details of the notions of juridical science in the strict sense and juridical prudence.

4.   The Formal Aspect of Juridical Knowledge

The Church or the people of God have a juridical dimension in which there is a juridical order that can and should be known, although it is not the only aspect of the Church. Through the juridical order we can establish a preliminary description of the specific nature of canonical science in a general sense. The object of juridical—canonical knowledge is the juridical aspect of the Church. That is the purpose of studying it and learning about it. But this is only a preliminary and negative way of delimiting juridical—canonical knowledge. It tells us that canonical science does not study other aspects of the Church as its proper objects, and it does not study the juridical aspect of civil society or of non-Christian religious communities; but it tells us nothing more. This criterion would be valid only if no other science were devoted to the juridical aspect, for from the moment that there is no juridical aspect, other criteria have to be used.

One thing we must remember. Since sciences are particularized by their typical way of conceptualizing (*modus definiendi et enunciandi*) or by the formal perspectives of conceptualization, the juridical aspect of the Church can be the exclusive object of canonical science only i if it is cognoscible or can be grasped in a single form of conceptualization, that is, from a single level of abstraction and from a single aspect. But is that the case?

It is indisputable that the juridical aspect of a society is generally not the object of a single science. Law is an object of study and learning by philosophy. Law can be studied from the sociological point of view. It can be learned about theologically (*sub ratione Deitatis* and according to the light of Revelation). It can be studied from the angle of political science, as an instrument of order and government, etc. The juridical dimension of the people of God is also the object of various sciences, although naturally in different ways. The juridical dimension may be studied by dogmatic theology, according to its own mode of conceptualization. It can be the object of morality insofar as it binds the conscience of the faithful. It can be the object of pastoral care, as an instrument of the action of pastors, etc.

However, none of these ways of studying and learning about the law of the Church gives us specifically juridical—canonical knowledge. When we say that a jurist is a man of law, or that a canonist is a technician of the ecclesial and just social order, we are referring respectively to the study of law or of canon law from a particular perspective. That perspective is *typical operativity* or the typical way in which the juridical concept operates in social life. What we have here is a consideration of the juridical dimension as something that, according to its nature, operates effectively, ordering the social life of a community of human beings. Thus typical operativity refers to the structuring and ordering action on social life by means of specific bonds, relationships, requirements and mandates.

We say *specific* because there are many bonds, requirements and mandates that are not the object of the science of law because they are not juridical. The juridical aspect is limited by the note of strict justice, equality and intersubjectivity. Intersubjectivity, or otherness, according to many authors, means the relationship of human beings with each other, a relationship that is dominated by the feature of exigency which is the binding force. This requirement arises immediately from the position of each person with respect to the others, like something inherent in the respective positions in the social environment or in the relationships among the positions. And these are not the bonds that exist between human beings and God.

Now we have described the limits of the formal aspect (formal object *quod*) of juridical knowledge: human sociality seen *sub ratione iuris*, or what amounts to the same, *sub ratione iustitiæ*. In other words, we are speaking of when juridical knowledge is presented as a requirement of persons with respect to other persons, either because of their personal condition or because of their social condition. Saying that we have delimited the formal aspect of juridical knowledge is equivalent to saying that we still need to indicate the final and specifying element: the formal perspectives of conceptualization. That is true, but since the specifying element operates at different levels of abstraction, it means that juridical—canonical knowledge in general has various degrees or levels with the common characteristics that have been indicated above.

5.   *The Different Levels of Juridical–Canonical Knowledge*

There are four levels of knowledge about juridical reality in the Church that we can identify in accordance with most recent philosophical juridical doctrine: *fundamental, scientific* or canonical science in the strict sense, *casuistic* and *prudential*. Of these four, only the first two are science properly speaking (knowledge through cause, with general validity). The difference between the fundamental and scientific levels lies in the fact that the fundamental level operates in the plane of *ontological* abstraction, whereas the scientific level operates as a *phenomenological* abstraction.

a) The epistemological nature of the fundamental level is determined by its operating on the abstract plane of ontological knowledge, but it is illuminated by the light of Revelation and its object is the people of God's natural and supernatural social realities. The fundamental level studies ecclesial juridical reality as requirements of Christians and of the Church, because of its nature, essence and qualities, that is, in accordance with the formal object of juridical knowledge. Juridical knowledge at the fundamental level explains and includes juridical *ontology* (the most intimate being and the ultimate causes of juridical—canonical reality) and juridical *axiology* (value judgments). It takes the form of a typical degree of juridical knowledge that is different from other types of knowledge because it operates on a different plane of abstraction; therefore juridical knowledge is conceptualized, defined and expressed in its own distinctive way. That leads to the creation of concepts, to the adoption of a notional lexicon, to judgments and proposals, and to the use of a certain method, all of which are typical. Although the terms used at the fundamental level may be identical at times to the terms used at other levels, the conceptual content—that is, the idea they express—is different.

It is this formal perspective of conceptualization and the methodology that make juridical—canonical knowledge autonomous and unique. As a knowledge readily obtained, it exists scattered throughout magisterial texts, theological works, writings on canon law, etc. But doctrine has not yet drawn up a scientific corpus as has, for example, the philosophy of law (with which it is not to be confused, although it takes some elements therefrom). Furthermore, there are many canonists who appear not yet to have realized that this is an autonomous type of knowledge. They have been rightly accused of indiscriminately mixing philosophical, theological, moral and juridical elements in their works, with the consequent confusion of substance and methodology. One of the reasons supporting the accusation is that they forget the uniqueness of the fundamental level. For example, to cite Saint Thomas's definition of law or the Suárez' definition of subjective law (at an ontological level) and say that these are definitions of law or subjective law at a scientific level is to confuse cognoscitive levels; such confusion is incorrect in good gnoseology. Similarly, when a magisterial or pastoral document, such as conciliar documents, speaks, for example, of the rights or duties of the faithful, these are nearly always notions obtained at the fundamental level (requirements for a Christian life, for example), and do not always or necessarily mean a right or duty in the technical—juridical sense. They may be requirements that in good juridical technique are included in diverse technical concepts or instruments: juridically protected interests, procedural norms, guarantees, particular ways of organizing the ecclesiastical hierarchy, etc. The same caution should be used in reading the writings of many tradition-oriented canonists.

Hopefully this science, which could be called the fundamental theory of canon law, will soon find specialists in whose hands it will become a consistent and well formed scientific body of knowledge.

We can inquire if the fundamental level is necessary for a complete knowledge of juridical reality in order to implement it. The response can be none other than affirmative. Because of its configuration, the social dimension of the people of God has inherent in it certain principles of order, requirements and values. In this sense, Christian life has requirements that arise from being the true Son of God; a Christian has a *dignitas* that implies certain personal values, and autonomy (*libertas*); a priest has a deep-seated mission to achieve; the Church has its own typical characteristics, etc. It is not therefore possible for the law to implant a truly just social order if the inherent nucleus of order is not known and respected, for the inherent nucleus is truly a just and social order. But learning about the inherent order is the proper business of the fundamental level, because we need to know the intimate essence, nature, values and order of reality, that is, juridical ontology and axiology. And it can be learned only at the abstract level of fundamental theory. The fundamental level studies both the natural and divine—positive juridical order, and also positive human law, but obviously, from its own perspective. That is why it does not study positive law *technically*, but *ontologically*, in its most deeply rooted final causes, that is, its essence, function, justification and assessment. Thus it tends to grasp the juridical reality of the people of God at the ultimate roots.

b) The second level of juridical knowledge is the *scientific* level. Here we have the *science of law* in the strict and most proper sense.

Juridical science is characterized as a *phenomenological* knowledge. Because it is a science, it asks about causes, but its purpose is not to grasp the final causes, which explain juridical reality as a whole (final causes are the purpose of the first level). Juridical science is concerned only with proximate and apparent causes ("apparent" means a cause that can be empirically grasped, for example, a promulgated law, or custom, a judicial decision, a contract, etc.). It is distinguished by the particular kind of analysis that it uses in conceptually determining juridical—canonical reality; that is, by its formal perspective of conceptualization. A little further on, its characteristics will be explained in greater detail.

c) The third level, which is not properly a science or is scarcely considered to be one, is represented by *juridical casuistry*.

Saying that it is not a science or that it is scarcely a science is not meant pejoratively. We are trying to refer to the fact that it is not very theoretical or abstract, but because it is practical, it can be a useful tool in the world of law. To say, as some authors have said, that casuistry is the grave of true science is an obvious exaggeration.

The purpose of casuistry is not to analyze juridical reality in a theoretical way, but to *synthesize* conclusions derived from the preceding levels to settle possible cases (those that have taken place or have yet to occur) with all the circumstances that make them singular. Casuistry is abstract to a certain degree, since is does not resolve real situations (as does a judge who hands down a decision), but resolves *typical* cases, past or possible situations. Casuistry is a knowledge of types (it especially studies cases as types) and of essence; it is not immediately practical and existential.

d) These three degrees or levels exhaust juridical knowledge, which, while having a practical dimension, mainly deals with pure knowledge. But, as we have said, there is another level that basically consists of decisions, although knowledge is implied. Decisions apply law to real life, to particular situations that really exist. This level of juridical knowledge concerns the act of legislating, judges' decisions, fulfilling a duty, exercising a right, or acting in accordance with justice and the law. This kind of *decision*, which is neither the conclusion of a logical syllogism or an arbitrary act of the will, is the result of a virtue (law belongs to the scope of that which is doable): juridical prudence.

The prudential level is not at all abstract or generic. It is an implementing knowledge, immediately practical, which introduces just decisions that organize society in real life. Such decisions are made at an absolutely unique moment that is irreplaceable and unsubstitutable. The characteristics of the prudential level are *immediate practicality* and *synthetic knowledge* because theoretical knowledge is applied to real-life situations with all their particular circumstances.

6.   *Autonomy and Interconnection Among the Different Levels of Juridical Knowledge*

Each of the levels of juridical knowledge studied is characterized by its particular formal perspective of conceptualization. The prudential level must be excepted because we cannot strictly speak of conceptualization since there is no degree of abstraction. But therein lies its specific difference.

An important consequence of the different perspectives is the autonomy of each level. Scientific autonomy means that each particular science (each level) has its own method and specific conceptual apparatus that correspond to a formal perspective or manner of intellectually harmonizing with juridical reality. Each science has in itself the necessary tools to reach the truth from its own perspective. In that sense, fundamental theory and canonical science have a certain specific autonomy in relation to each other, as has prudential decision, as we shall see at the appropriate time.

But also, none of these levels of knowledge can claim to be exclusive because each is totally insufficient to know and implement the entire juridical order. Each gives us one perspective, one view—or more precisely, one version, since understanding is not purely passive; and so we have different conceptualizations—of the truth of the object, which is not the whole truth.

The basic insufficiency of each of the levels of juridical knowledge shows the need for a connection between them. The connection appears in their orientation towards applying the law, in the note of practicality that at one stage or another is proper to all levels of juridical knowledge. In all of them there is a continuity of tendency and direction. But above all, the fact that there are different levels indicates that juridical reality cannot be approached at any one level alone and that an integral implementation of the social order requires a knowledge of juridical reality at all levels, held together by the same connection and in the existential oneness of the cognoscente.

It could be thought that the connection consists of the fact that they are levels of the same knowledge and not of different kinds of knowledge. This proposal does not account for the fact that each level has its own typical method of conceptualization, its own formal perspective of conceptualization, and that is precisely what formally distinguishes each from the others and particularizes each kind of knowledge.

Thus we have distinctions and autonomy, due to the incapability of the human mind to know juridical reality in its entirety, but only from different perspectives, in different modes of conceptualization and by different methods. And we have the necessary connection, because the thing that is learned about is one and the same object. These two characteristics must not be overlooked, just as one cannot be downplayed in favor of the other without incurring an incorrect gnoseology.

How does each level operate with respect to the others? By *data*, which are the truths that serve as the point of departure but which do not become a part of a different level from the level where they were obtained except through conceptualization and treatment in accordance with the perspective and method proper to each type of knowing.

Accordingly, there are two errors that must be avoided. The first is methodological confusion and the indiscriminate use by one science of the concepts and results obtained by another science. The second is converting the autonomy of the different levels into self-sufficiency, proposing or following a total methodological purity. On the other hand, scientific rigor and the needs of knowledge require *formal methodical purity*; it does not consist in ignoring the data from other sciences, but in not using the methods of other sciences, in not pursuing the study of the objectives belonging to other sciences, and in not indiscriminately transferring results from one science to another.

7.   Canonical Science

Science is the name given to the knowledge of something through its causes (*cognitio certa per causas*). With this meaning of the word science, few fields of knowledge merit the name better than philosophy, and within philosophy, metaphysics. But in modern times, especially from the 19th century onwards, one specific type of knowledge that has been truly developed in the last two centuries is called science by antonomasia; it is phenomenological knowledge, that is, knowledge that tends to grasp the object through its proximate causes and apparent qualifiers. The epistemological characteristics of this kind of knowledge differ substantially from ontological knowledge (which is proper to philosophy or to the fundamental level). Thus the philosophy/science contrast is frequently made, as if they were two specifically different kinds of knowledge. When in the preceding section we distinguished between the fundamental level and the scientific level, we were indicating that the fundamental level tsends towards ontological knowledge, whereas the scientific level is a phenomenological type of knowledge. This implicitly allows for a scientific knowledge (*cognitio certa per causas*) that is different from ontological knowledge. At the same time it means that we can name this cognoscitive level as juridical science, the scientific level, etc., using the terms in this restricted sense.

The development of juridical science strictly speaking can be said to begin with the historical school (Savigny, Puchta, Eichhorn, etc.); it received a strong impulse with Ihering and German dogmatics (Windscheid, Giercke, Enneccerus, Laband, Jellinek, etc.). The fundamental contributions of Roman jurisconsults were the basis of continental law for centuries and were mostly in jurisprudence, in its day a monument without peer to juridical prudence and technique. Glossators, commentators and others who were lawmakers and canonists[11] in the great medieval schools

---

11. For a study of the origins of canonical science and its history up to the Second Vatican Council, cf. J. HERVADA and P. LOMBARDÍA (†), *op. cit.*, note 1, pp. 189–225. Cf. also the following, among others: A. DE LA HERA, *Introducción a la Ciencia del Derecho canónico*, Madrid, Tecnos, 1967; J. FORNÉS, *La ciencia canónica contemporánea (Valoración crítica)*, Pamplona, EUNSA, 1984; E. MOLANO, *Introducción al estudio del Derecho Canónico y del Derecho Eclesiástico del Estado*, Barcelona, 1984; P. ERDÖ, *Introductio in historiam scientiæ canonicæ*, Rome, Edit. pontificia Università Gregoriana, 1990 (Spanish version: *Introducción a la historia de la ciencia canónica*, Buenos Aires, Educa, 1993, trans. M. D. Alonso o.s.b. and S. Dubrowsky).

contributed important technical improvements and established ideological bases of exceptional interest, noted down how to express basic concepts and, most of all, harmonized philosophy and medieval cultural ideals with juridical technique and the application of the law. Based on Saint Thomas's reflections on the ontology of law, scholastic philosophy took a great step forward in the philosophic knowledge of the juridical system (for example, the contributions of Suárez, Vitoria, Molina, etc.) in a powerful effort to give a Christian view of juridical reality. They studied everything from the essence of law to contracts, succession problems and international relations.

But all this scientific effort operated mostly on a philosophical—theological level, with a practical tendency that imprinted upon it a preoccupation with the morality of human acts. From there efforts moved forward almost without a break in continuity to technique, casuism and jurisprudence. *Ars iuris* was the domain of jurists and canonists, although they also adopted scientific methods from philosophers, theologians or moralists, or from phenomenology, or used textual criticism. However, even though there was a not-very-developed phenomenological knowledge, until the 19th century *scientia iuris* was thought of as one of the practical parts of moral philosophy or theology. Even attempts to study natural law *methodo mathematica o scientifica* (for example, Pufendorf, Wolff) that in some way implied a rupture with the metaphysical foundation of law did not intentionally depart from the philosophical level. *Scientia iuris*, the knowledge of law as different from juridical practice and technique, as we have just said, was considered to be a subordinate science, not an independent science; it was taken to be a *part* of a branch of philosophy, or in this case (canon law) a *part* of a branch of theology.

For a set of knowledge to be considered a science proper, in addition to autonomy, it must have certain epistemological characteristics that generally can be summarized in the definition indicated above: *cognitio certa per causas*. But it must also be a systemized set. This means the subject matter must be logically arranged (external systemization). Principally, as a consequence of its epistemological nature, it must deal with knowledge obtained in accordance with its own principles and its own conclusive procedure (a line of argument). All of which yields types of knowledge that are linked together and become a scientific system or harmonious set of types of knowledge (the internal systemization or system in its proper sense). Then the multiplicity of knowledge can be unified in a single kind of knowledge: a science.

The birth of juridical science as an independent area of knowledge distinct from philosophy (now we are dealing with the science/philosophy distinction) took place when a system of knowledge appeared that had been obtained not from philosophy, but from phenomenology. Juridical science could legitimately claim autonomy because the epistemological level at which this knowledge was reached is different, and the formal perspective of conceptualization (the *modus enunciandi et definiendi*) is distinct. That was the origin of a juridical science that is in no way a part of moral philosophy; in our case, we can say a canonical science that is in no way a part of moral theology.

Juridical science, the *new science* of law, taken at the phenomenological level, makes the following assumptions: a) it concerns knowledge and not just technique; b) the knowledge is general and valid without being tied to the contingency of the particular; c) it has its own principles, an internal linkage of knowledge and their reduction to one unit (the juridical system); d) knowledge of juridical reality is limited to observed and observable phenomena, that is, the juridical reality in its positivity and ability to be grasped phenomenologically without the need to know them at a philosophical level. All of which implies certain *explanatory* and *interpretive* rules that are typical of and proper to this level; in other words, juridical science needs a juridical method that is free of philosophical contamination or deviations. The construction of a juridical science with these characteristics has been the work of the new juridical science begun by the Historical School and with the introduction of the modern scientific or systematic method.

However, parallel to what has happened in the natural sciences, this process has not been free of exaggeration or of the "tragic error" of which Maritain speaks. Traditional science did not know how to discover the autonomy of the scientific level—or could not, since human nature is subject to the law of progress—and reduced it to a part of philosophy or theology; but the new science confused autonomy with independence, positivity with the denial of any philosophical foundation (which some currents of thought wanted to substitute with the *Allgemeine Rechtlehre* or general theory of law) and with ignorance of natural law. All of that led to conceptualism, positivism, formalism and to overlooking juridical prudence. All of those errors explain the climate of suspicion that arose in certain sectors at the end of the last great war, but which cannot take away our confidence in the total validity of juridical science understood as phenomenological knowledge.

The epistemological characteristics of juridical science, and therefore, of canonical science, can be indicated in the following way:

a) *The subject matter or material object* that canonical science deals with is, or may be, all of juridical reality insofar as it is empirically observable. Saying all of juridical reality implies saying that the subject of canonical science includes both divine law and human law.

A comment is necessary at this juncture. Leaving aside the problems that natural law may present in civil law because they are not properly dealt with here, it is not admissible to reduce the subject of canonical science to human positive law as some authors claim. For them, juridical science would study only positive human law, and theology would be the science proper to divine law. Such a position represents a confusion between the material object and the formal object of the sciences. Those authors forget that various sciences may study the same material object, but they are differentiated by the formal perspective of conceptualization and by the formal object. Divine law is the object of theology as it is theologically comprehensible, and it is the object of juridical science to the degree that it is or can be juridically understood, that is, from the perspective of canonical science. Deducing the content or formulation of divine law as it is known at any given moment in time is not the job of the canonist *as such* (personally, a canonist may be as good a theologian as any other). It is the function of the Magisterium, of theologians and of the Christian people, each according to its own function. But the study of that content as a current law and as elements of the juridical system is proper to canonical science. An example will make this clear. Saying whether a bishop has the power of jurisdiction by divine law or not is a statement that should be scientifically established by theology, and that is the purpose of its mission. On the other hand, determining whether that norm of divine law takes the form of strictly personal powers, or if the powers belong to a bishop as an *institution* of the Church is a conceptualization that belongs to canonists. A theologian is as ill-equipped to make such a determination from his scientific perspective as a canonist is to deduce the content of Revelation from his scientific perspective. Each, the theologian and the canonist, makes a complementary contribution.

b) The *mental approach* of canonical science, which completely conditions its typical manner of conceptualizing, affirming or defining, depends upon the aspect of juridical reality that the scientific level is trying to unveil; namely, that set of data that is being observed phenomenologically. Canonical science should consider the law in its peculiarities in order to describe it analytically and exegetically. Canonical science is not limited to description but tends *to express juridical concepts* that are obtained by an increasingly broad and abstractive generalization of the contents observed while they are in force in social life. To do that, a canonist should tend to know and point out the immanent purposes of the canonical system as a principle of interpretation; only through their purposes can the norms being analyzed make sense.

Here again a few comments are in order. First, the purposes to which we have just alluded are not the ultimate or transcendent ends of canon law (what in other places we have called ultimate or mediate ends). Those ends are accounted for as *data*, but knowledge and confirmation of them do not belong to this level as they are proper to the fundamental level described above. On the other hand, immanent ends are not only juridical ends, but also cognoscible and directly comprehensible by juridical science. (By immanent ends we mean the specific organizing direction of social life as a good or value to which a norm tends with its own ends, also called immediate ends, pieces of a just social order.) Renard was correct when he said that in law the ends are a part of the same science. This is true, but the ends are a part of sciences according to the epistemological nature that is proper to each science. And in juridical science, it depends upon the degree of phenomenological abstraction. In addition, although conceptualism and formalism have fallen into the defect of making an abstraction of the ends, as have some canonists, it is no less true that Ihering defended the fact that law is produced by reason of the end or purpose. Modern teleological or finalistic methods have proved him right.

The second comment refers to concepts. These are notions obtained at the phenomenological level and they are therefore typical of that level. They are not to be confused and cannot be confused with notions obtained at the fundamental level. They show juridical reality to a certain degree of cognoscibility (see *infra*, C, 2).

The third comment is doubtless the most important and most difficult to clarify. It refers to the note of *positivity* that the law must have in order to be scientifically studied. In good gnoseology it cannot be denied that canonical science—in general, juridical science—studies law only as positivized law.

Regardless of whether we are speaking of law or of the physical or natural sciences, any scientific study is phenomenological because by definition it is applied to what is empirically observable, to what is called a *phenomenon* (the given, insofar as it can be experienced). This is not questioning the existence of natural law, for example; it is strictly an epistemological problem. From that point of view, the response presents no doubt; only *positivized* law—not to be confused with human law—can be the object of juridical science by virtue of its epistemological characteristics: only positivized law is empirically observable.

Does that mean that canonical science does not study divine positive or natural law? No, as we have said; it means only that it studies divine law after it has become *manifest* and consequently is known as divine by the Christian community. As we know, the supernatural divine order of the Church passes through three moments, two of which interest us now: the *constitutive moment* or *supernatural eternal law,* and the *manifested moment,* one of the aspects of which is the progressive ecclesial awareness of the divine order. This awareness takes place historically and progressively as the Church and the faithful, learning to know one another, continue to unveil the mystery of salvation. So long as there is any element of divine law that has not yet become manifest, that no one is aware of, it is obvious that canonical science cannot make it an object of study. Nor is it the mission of canonical science to make it manifest. Unveiling the supernatural order, as we have said, is also not the exclusive mission of theological science. It is the task of the Magisterium, of the *sensus fidei* of the Christian people and of the work of theologians, each according to its proper function; and in juridical knowledge it is the mission of fundamental theory.

This gnoseological limitation in no way prevents canonical science from being sufficient for its object, which is the study of current law. Until the Church is aware of it, a norm of divine law is not, properly speaking, *law in force* and it is not a part of the normative social order that at any given moment in time governs the Church. Can one truly say—if the words actually mean anything—that a norm of divine law, today totally unknown and perhaps to be known after the next two hundred years, is today a part of the law in force? To reply positively would be to forget one of the essential characteristics of the law: its historicity. The law is not an ideal nor a prototype; it is a *practical and historical* system; that is, it is applicable *hic et nunc*. Everything else belongs to the law that should be, not to the law that is. And juridical science is a *practical* science, as we have said; its object is an operable order; and an unknown ideal cannot be seriously considered as such. If there is no operability or applicability, there is no law in force for juridical science, which is practical.

Positivization is the name we give to the process by which a juridical system passes into *historical existence*. But that does not mean that divine law should be included as a part of human positive law to be considered positivized. Any means available to the Church to make the progressive ecclesial awareness of divine law happen is a channel for positivization, each in its own way. Among the channels are *sensus fidei*, assent of the Christian people, magisterial acts, authors' doctrine, human legislation, juridical decisions, etc. After positivization, then divine law may be the object of canonical science.

c) The *purpose* of canonical science is to draw up a harmonious system of knowledge that is logically structured (all science is system; see *infra*, B, 2); thus it is possible better to grasp and arrange the juridical reality being treated, so as to facilitate comprehension, interpretation and application. This is accomplished through the use of the concepts indicated above as regulating principles. This technical and practical purpose conditions and gives sense to all theoretical analyses that are proper to this level of knowledge.

8.   The Prudential Level

As we were saying, bringing about an effective just social order requires a decision. That is why the implementing moment of canon law is not limited to fundamental theory or canonical science. On the contrary, both tend toward an implementing decision, which, as a human act, is the result of a combination of will and understanding—wanting to and knowing how to achieve something. Will is oriented by justice as the good toward which the will tends; understanding is governed by prudence as a norm or virtue of doing good work.

When we previously spoke of the fundamental level and the scientific level we referred to knowing how to do something. Are not those two levels sufficient? Will the cognoscitive factors of the decisions not be the conclusions of canonical science? To both questions the answer must be no. The normative moment is not simply an application of divine law nor of the order inherent in ecclesial reality to which we have previously alluded. It is a *historical option* in which the legislator has a directive and creative function. Before the author of the norm (either the legislator or the community or anyone with a *ius statuendi*), theoretically there is a range of possibilities available because people are free to shape their destiny. Thus the act of issuing a norm involves a choice. The choice is, of course, conditioned by a number of factors, the principal ones being divine law and the nature of the things. It cannot be a voluntarist decision, as the doctrine of juridical voluntarism claims. On the contrary, it implies a knowledge of reality and of the conditioning factors, together with a desire for justice. Why a knowledge of reality? Because the ends toward which there is a tendency and the principles that must be applied make an immediate reference to a real situation. The actual situation is what must be socially and justly ordered and consequently, it must be ordered according to the nature of the situation and the moment in time. Accordingly, a legislative moment involves choice and adapting means and norms to reality. All of this is a process that does not belong to logic—speculative reason—but to practical reason; it is a *prudential* process, for the correct habit of working properly with practical reason is given the name of prudence. It is a part of political prudence that traditionally has been called *prudentia iuris*.

The same can be said of the application of law. Judicial decisions or any behavior in accordance with the law is also not the result of a logical process of speculative reason. Indeed, any norm issued by the legislator, including a *præceptum* or *ius singulare*—has a more or less abstract nature, depending on the case. First, and this especially affects laws, the legislator deals with and regulates general cases looking at what they have in common with each other. But a particular case or a real situation is not a general case nor an abstraction; it is a singular and unique fact that has the general characteristics covered by the norm, but it also has other characteristics and may not be a hundred-percent match with those general characteristics. Second, the legislator, or whoever issues the precept, does not plan the subject's action down to the nth degree. The norms are generally incomplete and need to be completed by the subject's prudence.

The legislator's juridical prudence does not exclude the prudence of those for whom the norm is designed; on the contrary, it includes it. Every norm, no matter how abstract and general, requires more or less *adaptation* to a specific case. That adaptation, however, is not arbitrary, but prudential; that is, it must be done according to the actual situation. It therefore implies the application of established law, but the law applied according to the actual conditions of social life.

The acts that make up the process of prudential juridical decision are deliberation, judgment and imperium. Deliberation and judgment are part of decision to the degree that decision is cognoscitive. Imperium is part of the decision process to the degree that decision is preceptive. In the legislation process, possible norms are investigated with deliberation; the most suitable norm is determined with judgment, and is imposed by imperium. In turn, in applying norms the applicable norm and various possibilities for adaptation are investigated with deliberation; the most appropriate norm and its adaptation for the specific circumstances is chosen with judgment, and finally the subject of the norm, acts in accordance with the law by imperium.

Although a prudential decision has an element of will, basically it is knowledge, a cognoscitive grasp of reality and of the applicable norm. The epistemological characteristics of the prudential level have been indicated above: immediate practicality and synthetic knowledge. A good part of its connection with the fundamental and scientific levels lies in this synthetic quality. The abstract requirements grasped by the understanding at an ontological level and the truths that are also abstract and general which are obtained at a scientific level are synthesized and implemented in a specific singular situation through prudential judgment. Abstract conclusions—those stripped of any material condition of specific existence which exist on a fundamental level or on a scientific level—are general in nature and thus not applicable to a specific situation without the intervention of prudential synthesis. This is not a logical conclusion like a syllogism, but a step from abstract principles to a specific decision in a synthesis of general and universal normative elements with the elements of a real and specific case. In this sense scientific construction perfects and ensures a prudential decision, but does not substitute for it.

Juridical prudence should have the following requisites, among others of lesser importance: experience, intuition, counsel, good judgment and timeliness. It also needs equity or virtue in resolving cases that go beyond common norms.

APPENDIX

The reader will have noticed that in these pages on the function of prudence in law, we have spoken about both the prudence of the legislator and the prudence of the jurist and, in general, of the recipient of the norm. This has seemed best to us. But it is worth explaining that the so-called juridical prudence or *iuris prudentia* in the strict sense is what refers to the jurist and, as the case may be, to the recipient of the norm. The prudence of the legislator is pastoral prudence, in the case of the Church, or political prudence, if we are referring to civil society. The prudence of the legislator is certainly not juridical prudence, but what the writers on the virtues call political prudence, and we use pastoral prudence to apply this expression to the ecclesiastical legislator.

B. The Juridical Method

1. Preliminary Considerations

If sciences are ultimately specified by the way they make statements and definitions, it is obvious that methods, procedures and tools of knowledge are of the greatest importance to all sciences and specifically to canonical science. It is the canonist who possesses the proper method of this science; and anyone who does not possess them is not a canonist, for even though a person may possess great juridical knowledge, that person is nothing more than an erudite. To be a canonist means above all to possess a certain mental habit, a criterion, a method.

The juridical method is distinguished by the typical way it expresses its concepts and by the way it achieves the purpose of the law. A jurist conceptualizes, reasons, judges and works in accordance with rules—with a method—that are different from those of other sciences. The method used is determined by the practical truth that the science of law tends to grasp and by the good that it is trying to achieve (a just social order).

The juridical method is not an ingenious invention; it is a strict necessity. Everything that we have been saying about the way human understanding operates demands it. The juridical aspect of human reality can only be fully and correctly grasped if understanding is sufficiently in harmony with reality and follows the rules which enable it to grasp juridical truth and contribute to building a just social order.

That necessary characteristic of the juridical method should lead canonists and jurists in general, to a scrupulously methodical rigor. Adopting methods, modes of conceptualization, expression and procedure that are proper to other sciences (for example, philosophy or moral theology) leads only to errors and imprecisions.

This is a point which should be seriously meditated upon by canonists and moralists in ecclesiastical culture. Is it acceptable to have treatises on morality and canon law, sometimes written by the same author, where only the title is different, as we have had occasion to note? Can good juridical technique accept the application of moral probabilism to the juridical interpretation of laws as if committing or not committing a sin were the criterion for living lawfully? The juridical method is not useful to the moralist, nor is the theological—moral method useful to the canonist. The confusion between morality and law leads only to errors, sometimes tragic errors. If that path is followed, fundamental rights may be denied to a Christian, who is morally obligated to respect authority; or the possibility of exercising a right is confused with the obligation to exercise it, and the moral and ascetic rules of the gospel are forgotten. The same can be said of speculative theology.

As a condition and premise, the first thing required by the juridical method is a *juridical criterion* or the *viewpoint of a jurist*. What is this viewpoint of a jurist? It is simply considering reality from the point of view of a just ordering of society (a just social order). Therefore, a jurist observes reality and its laws to the degree that they produce and achieve order. We are not speaking of just any kind of order, but specifically of an order based on the criteria of justice. And finally, a jurist does not consider reality and its laws from the point of view of an individual, but from a social point of view.

The second premise is a *formal methodical purity*. Canonical science is an *autonomous* science at the same time that it is dependent upon data from other sciences. Canonical science studies the social reality of the Church from its own perspective—social relations with nuances of intersubjectivity and justice—which is different from the theological perspective. Canonical science is, then, a distinct and autonomous science.

What does "autonomous" mean? Simply that canonical science has its own way of conceptualizing and its own method that are not taken from any other science. It is not a subordinate science; it is not a part, even a specific part, of any other science—of theology, for example. In other words, canonical science possesses sufficient tools to recognize the material object according to its formal object.

Autonomy, however, does not mean self-sufficiency nor does it preclude what is called the subordination of the sciences. On the contrary, juridical science, as we have said, requires data from other levels and other sciences because it is *insufficient* to capture all of reality.

Every human action finds its ultimate and most intimate organizational module in human beings and their ultimate purposes. That means that knowing human actions on a scientific plane sometimes requires knowing the principles that govern being and its ultimate ends. Thus philosophy, theology and, in a special way, fundamental theory must provide canonical science with the prior knowledge it needs to have. Those sciences should provide the information because juridical science, in accordance with the epistemological characterization described above, moves at an abstractive level and uses tools that do not grasp being and its ultimate ends.

Now, the *data* provided to canonical science are prepared with non-juridical tools, and the data are often obtained from a higher level of abstraction. This implies that the data have been stripped of the nuances that canonists need to take into account and that qualify conclusions when the data are applied to real life. Therefore, the *data* must be conceptualized and considered from a canonist's point of view so that a juridical conclusion may be drawn from them. This is, ultimately, an application of the normal process of knowing the science of law to the theological or philosophical data or the data from fundamental theory.

Perhaps an example will clarify what we have just said. Theology gives a notion of the sacrament of baptism that includes diverse elements such as the sign of a sacred thing, the production of grace, incorporation into the Church, instilled virtues, a sacramental character, etc. From all those elements the science of law will abstract the juridical notion of baptism: the juridical fact (or act, according to various authors) that incorporates a person into the Church. The juridical concept that explains the reality of baptism from the point of view of canonical science is not so much the sign as it is the juridical fact. The effect that interests canonists is not so much grace as it is juridical incorporation into the Church. In any case, the supernatural effect produced will interest canonists insofar as it causes—if indeed it does—any juridical effects.

Therefore canonists need the data that philosophers or theologians provide, but the data should not and cannot in good gnoseology be applied to law without being passed through the sieve of juridical criteria, and for a simple reason: they are data obtained by typical means of conceptualization that give a theological or philosophical view that is different from a juridical view, since the perspective of consideration is different.

Here it should not be forgotten that reality is one thing and the different degrees or levels of knowledge are another thing; consequently, no level or degree of knowledge is *exclusive*, only partial. It is also another thing that one person may have total knowledge of reality through different sciences and cognoscitive levels.

To be consistent with the gnoseology from which we started, we must conclude that each science works at a different abstractive level and from diverse perspectives of consideration. This implies not only the possibility, but the necessity, of pureness of method. But pureness is not total, only formal. In other words, a canonist cannot take into account only strictly juridical data (norms, decisions, rights, etc.), but often will have to have recourse to metajuridical realities and the data provided by other sciences. But those realities and data will be studied with a jurist's vision from the typical perspective of canonical science. In this way only data with *juridical relevance* will be taken, data that color or condition the juridical system or juridical acts, and they will be studied within canonical science using juridical methods—the only way that the result will also be juridical. If the data are studied using non-juridical methods, the lack of methodical rigor will invalidate or distort the results.

2.   *Exegesis and Construction of the System*

The process of scientifically constructing canon law includes two consecutive stages: *exegesis* and systematic construction or *systemization*.

Exegesis analytically studies laws so they can then be interpreted. Systematic or scientific construction enunciates principles, and relates, organizes and unifies the knowledge obtained.

It is in the systemization that the science of law reaches its highest level of science. As we know, the methods of construction and systematization tend to facilitate the organization of knowledge into *systems* or *theories* so that the connection of ideas matches the connection of things. When we remember that science is a set of truths that are logically linked together *in such a way as to form a coherent system*, it is easy to understand that the systematic or scientific method (systematic construction) gives canonical science its most deeply scientific quality. The purpose of the modern systematic method is not only to organize the subject matter logically (the old systematic method), but more importantly it is to unify and explicate the subject coherently by enunciating concepts and theories. The concepts and theories establish the principles, general characteristics and constants that justify the configuration of the system. That is why the scientific method is based on abstraction.

Exegesis and systemization are not incompatible with each other; on the contrary, they are complementary. Exegesis without system is a rudimentary and incomplete stage of science; systemization without exegesis is impossible.

An effort to discover the precise scope of the terms in which the legislator expressed himself and exactly what he had in mind for each norm (exegesis) is vital and must precede systemization. In this sense, the work carried out by exegetes is notably fertile; a scientist who attempts to collaborate in the task of systematic construction, far from belittling the effort of the exegetes, must keep it well in mind.

The task of constructing the system is the proper task of a scientist. The set of knowledge must be systematized and the relations that link the norms with each other must be explained by enunciating general concepts that give us the meaning of the rules and the key to making just decisions in individual cases.

APPENDIX

The systematic method considerably widens the field of the study of canon law, and so leads to *specialization*. This is a result of the fact that the systematic method implies *the distinction of branches*. Just as the exegetical method operates through the division of the study of canon law by *subjects* or subject criteria, the systematic method divides the study of canon law by *formalities*, by different formal perspectives of consideration; these formalities constitute the *branches* of canonical science.

Within the systematic method then, what does the distinction of branches represent?

The distinction of branches is born of the observation that, within the only juridical method and from a fundamental unity of perspective of conceptualization, there is a variety of ways to conceptualize and of principles and technical resources. Thus, for example, the subjective right does not always behave the same in the sphere of relations between private persons as in the sphere of public administration; within a fundamental unity, the subjective right has certain differences of exercise and defense in the constitutional, administrative and private spheres. In this way, by building the system, we build a series of subsystems or *branches of law*. Each of these branches is distinguished by its *particular principles* and it *characteristic technical resources*.

What are the branches of canon law? In my opinion, they are these: General Part, Constitutional Law, Law of the Person, Ecclesiastical Organization, Administrative Law, Criminal Law, and Procedural Law.

We might wonder: is the distinction of branches of any particular interest after the Code of 1983? In my opinion, it is of special interest. Let us consider, for example, the existence of associations and of private juridical persons; we clearly see here—together with the relevance of the personal charisms— the sphere of the private autonomy of the faithful and with it the need to take into account the principles that govern said autonomy. This leads to the building of the Law of the Person, based on the principle of private autonomy. The fundamental rights of the faithful postulate the construction of Constitutional Law and of Administrative Law. Moreover, the break in the class conception requires a change in the way we study the hierarchy, which, by being a treatment *de personis*, must become a discussion of the ecclesiastical organization, etc. I believe that without the distinction of branches, it would be difficult to implement all the potentialities of the *CIC* 83.

3.   Scientific Thought

Because the science of law is a phenomenological science it requires a scientific spirit and a positive spirit in persons who practice it. A scientific spirit must have the following qualities: a) *Objectivity*: The scientist must scrupulously submit to the object under study and make an effort to observe it as precisely as possible. That means eliminating any prejudice (the data provided from other fields does not constitute prejudice) and using all means of information and observation available. Objectivity is reflected in intellectual probity and in the spirit of observation. b) *Rigor*: A scientist should try not to state anything that is not rigorously demonstrated according to all the exigencies of the object. At the same time, something that has not been demonstrated by the scientific method may be accepted as true if it has been shown to be true in a higher field of knowledge (ontological knowledge). In that case methodical rigor requires that a conclusion of a different nature not be given as a scientific conclusion. c) *Critical spirit*: It is through a spirit of intellectual freedom that scientists accept that they must revisit established certainties, permit discussions and reservations, question the results of their investigations and always be ready to modify their own conclusions. One of the conditions of science is knowing how and when to doubt, for the passion for questioning increases with knowledge. It is a form of love of the truth, an awareness of the complexity of reality and of the limits of human intelligence (Jolivet).

The phenomenological nature of canonical science also calls for a positive spirit, which is determined by the following: a) *Submission to data*: Legal scientists must respect data in the sense that the objectivity that directs and organizes their studies is primarily a juridical phenomenon—juridical reality as a given and as phenomenologically observable. b) *Reduction to what is workable*: The truths that are reached must be translated into juridical formulas so they can be implemented. c) *The idea of functional intelligibility*: All juridical concepts and all theories are intelligible and valid to the degree that they are functional, meaning to the degree that they explain and facilitate the operation of the law. d) *The idea of scientific sufficiency*: The idea here is that every juridical phenomenon can be adequately explained (although not in its ultimate causes) by another juridical phenomenon. This assumes there will be no recourse to metapositives as an explanation of the phenomenon, for the proper explanation of juridical science should be phenomenological. But, as we have said, this does not prevent being open to data from ontological knowledge. On the contrary, that kind of knowledge is a *guide and contrast* for the scientific task. What we mean is that philosophical or theological explanations cannot be given as a scientific explanation. The scientific reduction to a systematic unity of juridical knowledge requires that *explanations* of the principles, of the relationship between consequences and constants, be obtained at the phenomenological level. That is the only way there can be a scientific system; otherwise it would be another type of system or no system at all—only a mere aggregation of different kinds of knowledge.

At first sight it may seem paradoxical that the application of the scientific approach to the continuous progress of different fields of knowledge through research should have found the university to be the best place to preserve it and stimulate it. We cannot forget, though, that universities are institutions designed for the continuous investigation of new scientific findings by applying rigorous and adequate methods. By their very nature, universities are a favorable environment for a continuing exchange of the most diverse ideas, for free expression of the most varied concerns, for raising the most open-ended questions. This could lead us to believe that the *scientific approach* and the *university spirit* are in contrast.

But the paradox is only apparent. Only someone open to any problem of interest presented by the broad field of human culture can really be dedicated to a specific scientific project and willingly accept a limited field of investigation with a rigorous scientific method as a personal occupation. If this combination of object and method is not the fruit of a voluntary decision to contribute new findings to the broad panorama of human culture, but is only the result of an inability to see beyond a minuscule piece of work, then the scientific investigation will scarcely be valid.

In addition, a preoccupation with cultural problems or a perhaps generous feeling for the more serious problems of humanity are no more than a sterile diversion for amateurs if the person completely lacks specific and rigorous experience with the scientific method. A balance between the two is perhaps the most glorious constant in the history of universities.

With regard to the subject of canon law and, generally speaking, all disciplines concerned with the Church, it is perhaps not superfluous to note that the great ideals of freedom and openness that seem to be bursting forth so vigorously in our times can be little served unless the rigor of scientific method is effectively applied in their service.

C. Tools of the Juridical Method

Now that the basic principles of method have been established, in the following pages we will try to give a succinct overall view of the tools used in the juridical method. As there are many, we shall limit ourselves to a significant few.

1. Abstraction in Legislative Technique and in Juridical Science

Legislative technique is based on abstraction. The task of the legislator would be unthinkable without abstraction; without it there would have to be a regulation for each individual case. Laws are possible because human understanding is capable of grasping and abstracting the common qualities in certain groups of beings, individual facts or acts, reducing them to a representative form and making a judgment about them that is applicable to all of them. For example, from all individual marriages, taken together, there is born the concept of "marriage." From the inherent value of each human being, the idea of "human dignity" is deduced.

This is the process that makes laws possible. The legislator takes the common characteristics of groups of acts, social structures or things, and regulates them in a law through a judgment about them. Thus every law is always a general and abstract norm that must be prudently applied.

In the same way, because the science of law is a science (knowledge with general validity), it acts by abstraction. It studies office, marriage, parish priests, sale of property, or the various types of associations.

What are the qualities of abstraction? First, there are the qualities that are common to all types of abstraction (we are referring to the predicamental abstraction). Depending upon the degree, abstraction is a more or less intense process of separation from the material conditions of the particular existence of an object. Knowing a set of objects, the mind separates out the qualities that are predicable of each one, and keeps only the ones that are predicable of all. From a set of acts of worship with common characteristics comes the notion of sacrament, for example. In that sense, each abstract notion "impoverishes" the object because abstraction takes from it that which makes it specific. That is how the concept arises; it is made up of the set of qualities that the mind collects together into a single idea, after discarding the other qualities that are not relevant to this case. What is the criterion that causes the interest for these qualities and so for this type of concept? For our purposes we can say that the interest is based upon the formal aspect in which we are operating and the perspective that illuminates the object. For example, man is a living being, an animal, a human composed of a body and soul, a citizen, a faithful Christian, a friend, a sick person, etc. Each of these concepts is applicable to a human being, but all of them indicate only a few of the characteristics. The greater the degree of abstraction, the "poorer" the concept; that is, the fewer qualities the concept takes from the abstracted object. However, at the same time, it applies to a greater number of objects. Thus "man" can be applied to every human person, but "faithful Christian," a richer concept because it includes the concept of man plus the fact of belonging to the Church, is predicable of a smaller number of people. The process of abstraction is applicable to juridical science, which also acts through abstraction because it indicates specific qualities of reality.

Second, as we have said, the degree of abstraction in canonical science is not strongly *philosophical* (ontological or substantial); it is an empiriological or accidental abstraction inherent to science (the scientific level to which we have referred). This kind of abstraction, by using a procedure that compares phenomenologically observed aspects, tries to enunciate the unified concepts or outlines that are needed to achieve the technical purpose being pursued: the best organization, comprehension and application of the law (Ferrer Arellano). However, at this level there is also a gradation of abstraction; thus, as we have said, concepts of varying breadth may be accommodated.

Finally, the concepts, judgments and statements obtained by canonical science are law-specific; that means that jurists abstract the elements from reality that reflect the mode of reality that belongs to the order of law and that is different from other sectors of reality. Thus arise the juridical concepts, judgments or statements that reflect a certain *aspect* of the truth—the aspect that must be known in order to establish a just social order. If a jurist or legislator issues a judgment ("such and such an action is lawful," for example), the lawfulness refers to behavior that can be juridically evaluated and not exactly to a moral evaluation, which might be different. Saying moral evaluation is also saying technical evaluation of another type.

2.   *Juridical Concepts*

Because the science of law operates with abstractions, it normally makes use of concepts (intellectual representations of things). Many of its concepts are taken from other sciences or from everyday thinking (for example, baptism, man). In those cases the content and value of the concepts are the same as in the original sources.

But at other times, juridical science creates its own concepts, which are *juridical concepts*. How are these concepts formed?

a) Some simply come from delimiting or fixing concepts taken from other sources for technical—juridical needs. Take, for example, the term "domicile," a notion that theoretically means the place where a person lives with a certain degree of permanence. But domicile is a concept without fixed contours; using it indiscriminately would cause considerable difficulties in applying laws that refer to it or that involve it. Therefore, juridical technique delimits the concept and gives it some fixed qualities, even distinguishing between domicile and quasi-domicile.

b) Other concepts that may not come from juridical science are typically conceptualized in law. They are stripped of irrelevant connotations and other connotations may be added; for example, good faith.

When the concepts listed heretofore pass into juridical science, they retain their original qualities—except of course, for those that are stripped away when they are conceptualized by juridical science—regardless of the degree of abstraction with which they were obtained. Thus concepts with a value that is translated into requirements preserve their normative content and may serve as the basis for decisions, as Coing states, although always according to the nature and technique of law.

c) Finally, there are a number of juridical concepts that originate in juridical thinking and knowledge, although they have passed into other sciences or into the common language (contract, subject of law, declaration of wishes, local Ordinary, administrative act, etc.). Scientific construction is mainly based on this type, which may be called the *basic concepts* of juridical science. Those concepts are the ones that are construed in full accordance with the level of abstraction at which the science of law works. They may thus be considered to be pure juridical concepts; all others are concepts that have been adopted.

All juridical concepts, pure or adopted, may be classified as follows:

- essential concepts based on ethical values; for example, good faith or scandal in canon law;

- essential concepts based on social phenomena of given value, such as a person, or the conjugal community of life;

- general empirical concepts of things or facts that are important in social life; immovable goods, for example;

- concepts that are empirical (because of the level at which juridical science operates) but also have a technical—juridical nature; for example, an object of law or an administrative act.

As we have said, value concepts have a normative content; others, such as general empirical and purely juridical concepts, have only a delimiting value.

Like all concepts, from the point of view of their connotations, juridical concepts can be classified as *higher* or *lower*. Lower concepts are contained in higher concepts; thus the subject of law is a higher concept that also contains the physical person and the moral or juridical person; juridical business includes contracts, wills, etc. Higher concepts have fewer features than lower concepts and therefore have greater scope.

Logically, all features included in a higher concept are predicable from the lower concepts. In juridical science, however, that is not always the case because of the epistemological nature of the concepts, which are obtained more by generalizing than by universalizing. In many cases, a certain feature may express the general characteristics of a group of facts or acts that may at times contain exceptions. Still, often the exception reveals a defect in systematization. This is a correctable error in scientific work, but not in laws that are in force, unless they are amended. Thus an interpreter must keep this anomaly in mind because excessively conceptualizing a generality could lead to unsatisfactory results that are contrary to the spirit of the laws.

Here we can point out the error sometimes incurred by using defective concepts in an argument either in the juridical description of facts or acts or in applying certain features to them. An illustrative example might be the argument used by some authors when describing marriage as a contract or not. Sometimes the features t hat show it is a contract and do not make it a marriage are actually features of the "contract," but they express a concept that is merely a type of juridical act and is different from the type applicable to marriage. On the other hand there are a good number of theologians or canonists who forget that the concept of contract they are dealing with was substituted some years ago in general theory by juridical act or transaction, and they call a juridical transaction a contract. Some are using a lower concept and some a higher concept. The result is a dialogue of the deaf.

One quality common to all juridical concepts is their technical and instrumental nature. In adopted concepts this quality is limited to aspects that are the object of juridical conceptualization; in pure juridical concepts it includes all features.

The technical and instrumental nature of juridical concepts is a consequence of the nature and purpose of juridical science. Juridical science does not tend to tell us what things are, in an ontological sense, but what they presuppose or what function they have in the juridical system. It does not try to learn what a human being is, for example, or what a sacrament or a temple is; that is a task for philosophy, theology, liturgy or architecture. Juridical science tries to learn what these realities represent or what function they have in the world of historical and current law. When canonists write about a concept, for example, the rights of a subject, or moral person, they make no reference to the ultimate and basic ontology of any realities (that is a function of philosophy or the fundamental level, in the case of canon law); they refer to a living social system, to technical tools or modes of organizing that are based on criteria of truth and justice and that presuppose a historical option and a creative factor in the human mind. This is especially true for concepts that are not proper to or usable by legislation, but only by science, which tends, through the concepts, to organize and explain a certain juridical order. Concepts that are not useful for this technical purpose should not be constructed, nor should concepts that have lost their use be retained.

Pure juridical concepts are, or should be, true, but the truth they manifest is, after all, a technical truth; thence arise their relative and instrumental qualities. The qualities are relative because they reveal not the intimate essence of things but what they are and what they represent in a given juridical system, according to the technical criteria of organization proper to the system.

Does that mean there is no permanently valid juridical knowledge? No, it means that *absolute*, not relative, juridical knowledge is proper to the fundamental level; and, because of the degree of abstraction used and the purpose, the scientific level creates concepts that, together with features that may be absolute and permanent, contain other features that belong to specific legislation and are therefore variable, although in fact they do not vary. Here we must keep in mind that if a feature changes, the concept changes, although only with respect to the feature. It also means that the scientific level is a science mainly because it has developed methods that obtain rationally demonstrable knowledge (it is a science especially because of its method). This has been held by many modern authors (Larenz, De Castro, etc.). And finally it means that complete juridical knowledge requires several levels of knowledge.

3. Hypotheses and Theories

If juridical science involves reduction to a single unity, it cannot be limited to studying data nor, therefore, to conceptualizing data. It must find explanations and connections among the different kinds of data. In this task of explicating and constructing unity there arise *hypotheses* and *theories*.

A *hypothesis* is a provisional explanation of observed phenomena; its function is to coordinate known data (its systematic function) and to direct a scientist's work (its heuristic function). The sources of hypotheses are the following: intuition, dissociation and association of groups of data, and deduction. To be valid, a hypothesis must be simple, and suggested and verifiable by the data (Jolivet).

Strictly speaking, *theory* includes the explanations that unify other partial explanations. The whole juridical order, or great sections of it, is systematically constructed under the light of theory; examples are Kelsen's pure theory of law or the theory of juridical systems with which Italian constitutionalists have constructed their science. A theory is frequently based on a concept or a hypothesis. Theories coordinate and unify knowledge, and they are investigative tools.

Hypotheses and theories in juridical science are both instrumental and relative. They neither express nor explain the ultimate reality of law; they explain only the juridical phenomenon. That is why they cannot be directly translated nor applied to ontological explanations (philosophy, theology, fundamental theory). And that is why it is meaningless to criticize them from the wrong perspectives; they do not adequately serve those sciences. Such is the case, for example, of theologians who admit the institutional aspect of ecclesiastical jurisdiction but reject the applicability of the theory of the ecclesiastical body. Their arguments clearly show that they have fallen into this error. In effect, organic theory does not ontologically explain the intimate essence of the titularity of ecclesiastical jurisdiction; but that is because organic theory is a scientific theory, proper to canonical science and obtained phenomenologically. Consequently it explains, not the ultimate essence of the subject, but the reality of the juridical phenomenon. That reality escapes ontology, where theologians work when they raise the question and study it. It is quite a different matter not to admit organic theory because of not accepting the institutional aspect of jurisdiction or because of viewing it differently. And that is a point into which we shall not delve here.

4. Juridical Types

Another technical resource in juridical science is the use and delimitation of *types*. A type in juridical technique can be: a) a means of designating the suppositions of fact in norms; b) a form of comprehension and presentation of juridical relationships (Larenz).

This procedure has been taken by juridical science from general systems of thought. It is derived from either a generalization of the characteristics related to the frequency with which they occur (for example, a typical Frenchman, a typical Spaniard) or from an expression of a normative ideal (an ideal figure or type of Christian, religious, etc.) or from an expression of a representative average (the typical diligence of a good paterfamilias), etc.

a) To designate suppositions of fact, juridical technique uses frequently occurring types, which should be interpreted as such and not as they are expressed in other sciences or techniques. Juridical technique also uses normative average types, as in the case of determining the negligence of an officeholder; in those cases, the starting point is not the ideal diligence of a parish priest, for example, but the diligence of an average priest, whose behavior is considered as a point of contrast for the purpose of interpreting the law.

Normative ideal types, examples or archetypes such as the ideal of a Christian, a bishop, a parish priest, etc., as Larenz says, represent a *meta-image*. It is necessary to tend toward them, even though the ideal can never be reached in its full purity. The types become *criteria for assessment* in all kinds of behavior and situations. As ideal types they are metajuridical, although they may be described in a law (of higher rank and especial solemnity, otherwise it would make no sense); but they may also be used as criteria for the legitimacy of the content of laws and as criteria for assessing and applying laws.

b) The types of greatest interest for both legislative technique and scientific construction are the types that refer to the structure and configuration of actions, institutions and juridical relationships. How are these types treated? By virtue of some of the forms of "typification" that we have mentioned, from the great variety of actions, institutions or relationships in real life some are chosen that are considered typical at a given moment in time. The juridical structuring (the legislative moment) of those actions, relationships or institutions, or their explanation and systematic construction (scientific creation) are carried out accordingly. That is, legislation indicates the principal characteristics of the types and in accordance therewith regulates the realities with which it is dealing. With this procedure a "legal type" is created and shaped; for purposes of recognition and regulation, a type serves as a juridical channel for the entire set of realities that answer to that type.

The "legal type" typifies and configures the structure of certain actions, institutions or relationships and thus belongs to the class of types called *structural*. It is clearly distinguishable from frequently occurring types and the normative average types already cited. The legal type fulfills an instrumental technical function—being a channel for recognition and regulation—thus, it is not absolute in nature; that is, it serves to regulate the realities that answer to the type, but does not exclude others.

An epistemological nature is characteristic of the legal type, but it should not be confused with the epistemological nature of juridical concepts. The legal type, rather than being a juridical concept, is an *empirical outline*, a schematic reproduction of the structure of a reality that is considered to be "typical." In other words, to form a type, the mind does not conceptualize, it schematizes, making a prescientific abstraction. Therefore, the degree of abstraction is very slight and an immediate and proximate reference to reality is retained. That has an important consequence. As Larenz says, types must be created and interpreted in accordance with the substantial elements of reality (the nature and real content of the sector or form of regulated social life) that the type is schematizing.

That epistemological characteristic of types explains their use in juridical technique. When an action, relationship or institution fully answers to the characteristics of a type, it is recognized and regulated on that basis alone. If that does not happen because some of the characteristics are not the same, it is still recognized and regulated in accordance with the type, but at the same time there is recourse to specific law or to other technical resources so as to respect the differences.

The instrumental nature of types is significantly demonstrated in their use to give juridical viability to realities that—according to some established principle but not because of the technique of using types which is never exclusive—could not be juridically viable unless they fell into one of the types configured by the law. Thus, for example, given the principle of not admitting new forms of religious orders, which was in force for several centuries in the Church, the device used was to give the new forms juridical viability and approve them as associations of the faithful and grant them certain privileges. Thus to know the nature of a specific and singular reality, it is not enough to start with the legal type that enabled the new forms to be approved; specific law also has great importance. Of course, it should not be necessary to say that outside the world of law, what must be kept in mind is real substance. For example, for a theological study of religious life, the use of legal types is valid only to the degree that, as we have said, legal types schematize substantial elements. But it must not be forgotten that a legal type does not schematize all the realities found in a single concept, but only those realities that, either because they are so frequent, or through their characteristics or for other reasons, are at a given time considered as typical. Here indeed a theologian who tried to schematize them all could be called "juridistic" because this is a confusion of different methods and logically can lead only to unsatisfactory results. So long as theological and juridical methods are confused, the ecclesiastical sciences will have a great deal of confusion of language.

Juridical relationships, acts or institutions that can not be contained within the types configured by the law or by science are called *atypical* and are distinguished from typical forms or normal types. Atypical forms are not outside the law; they are regulated by any general norms there may be, by special laws or simply by specific norms.

Atypical acts, relationships and institutions are recognized as a normal phenomenon in social life and in juridical technique. However, in canonical doctrine—but not by the authorities—they are a phenomenon that has been scarcely taken into account or used. Possibly this is due to the persistence of a mentality that can be translated into a phrase attributed to Gasparri: "quod non est in Codice non est in mundo." This phrase evidently has nothing to do with either law or juridical science. The same is also valid for *CIC*.

Legal types may be *open* or *closed*. Open types include only some partial characteristics. Closed types completely delimit a figure and all its characteristics.

Delimitation of a legal type, as we have said, is based on a schematization of realities that under various criteria are considered as typical at a moment in time. Now, apart from the evolution that is natural to all law, there is a special evolution in the case of types. They can pass from open to closed, or be delimited in accordance with realities that become typical at another given moment. That may cause a substantial change or partial modification in the type. What then happens with realities that persist and are recognized and regulated according to a certain type? Normal technique gives an option to change the figure by which they are regulated. When that is not possible, the principles of acquired rights and the non-retroactiveness of the laws are taken into account. All of this concerns the technique of types. It is different when a change or modification obeys other criteria; for example, when an attempt is made to modify substantial reality. But this attempt is only possible, obviously, if the authorities are competent to make it; that is not the case, for example, if the fundamental rights of the faithful are at stake. To close, let us make clear that it is one thing to change or modify a type and something else to change or modify the norms that regulate the evolution of the realities that are included therein.

5.   Simplifying by Reduction

This tool of the juridical method consists of substituting a quantity for a quality.

Social reality sometimes has fluctuating boundaries and does not obey set rules, but it has qualities that should be taken into account by the law. Then it is necessary to adopt fixed criteria that are both just—suitable for reality—and sure. In those cases one of the resources used by juridical technique is to reduce a quality to a quantity.

The Decr. *Christus Dominus*, for example, includes the resignation of bishops "if due to advanced age they become less able to fulfill their duties." If the norm had remained in that form, the difficulties and controversy that each case could lead to are evident. What would the criteria be for measuring the diminished capabilities of each bishop? Would they be related to the time of appointment? Would they depend upon the average capability of all the bishops in the world, all the bishops on a continent or in a country, etc.? How would "advanced age" be determined? As a just and prudent norm it is virtually inapplicable, unless the decision were left to the bishop in question, as the Decree finally actually did. In cases like this, the process of simplifying by reduction comes into play. Advanced age and diminished capability, which are qualities, are transformed into a quantity, which is the seventy-five years of age found in c. 401.

Thus any questions that could be raised are eliminated from the start. Other examples of the principle are majority of age, prescription, etc.

6.   Formal Equivalents and Juridical Fiction

Formal equivalents, also called remissions or references, are a basic resource for legislative technique. To avoid superfluous repetition, *for juridical purposes* the law makes one factual presupposition equivalent in law to a different one. Equivalents are found in the *CIC* with expressions like *censeatur tamquam*, *æquiparantur* and *habeatur pro*. They essentially consist of a cross-reference from a norm to other norms that regulate factual patterns which are equivalent to those contemplated by the first norm.

A special type of formal equivalent is *juridical fiction*, which is due more to historical use and the language sometimes used than to its nature.

Juridical fiction originated in Roman law from the requirements of juridical traffic. In contrast to early quiritarian law, which was considered intangible, a procedure was used which *feigned* that a fact different from the one covered by law was the same, thus making them equivalent for juridical purposes. After the medieval acceptance of Roman law, following Roman technique, canonists and legists for centuries defined fiction as "legis adversus veritatem, in re possibile ac ex iusta causa dispositio" (Alciato). Although many canonists still define it this way, in modern times many others no longer admit that configuration (Reiding, Demelius, Ihering, Stammler, Esser, Legaz, etc.), or they call it a latent remission or latent equivalent (Larenz). Also from the point of view of canon law, the traditional definition has been subjected to revision (Llano Cifuentes).

Actually, the technique of juridical fiction does not feign anything, nor does it contain any untruths. It is a legislative device by which, as in any equivalence, the juridical effects of one fact are given to another. With Llano we can say that *fictio juris* is a tool of juridical technique by which, formally making two actually different presuppositions of fact to be equivalent, equivalent juridical treatment is achieved when the juridical effects that a different juridical norm gives one presupposition are given to a different presupposition.

APPENDIX

Two points about the *æquiparatio in iure*. This formal comparison is only characteristic of the legislative technique; it devolves upon the legislator and only upon him to establish it. It is then not a function of the interpreter. If the jurist is faced with two similar situations, one of which suffers from a gap in the legislation, he cannot establish a formal comparison, but must resort to analogy (c. 19 of the *CIC* 83 and also c. 17).

To establish the formal comparison, the legislator may resort to the general law, to the particular law or even to administrative acts.

The second point refers to the term *assimilantur* used in c. 368. Some writers have tried in this case to see a so-called distinction between *assimilation* and *comparison*. In this case, assimilation would exceed the limits of a juridical comparison to indicate a *substantial* similarity; it would try to say that communities similar to the dioceses, particular Church, are also, one way or another, particular Churches or at least would be similar to them. On this point, it is necessary to distinguish the theological problem from the juridical problem or the correct interpretation of the words of this c. 368. The theological problem of to what extent those communities are or are substantially similar to the particular Church, no doubt exists, but its resolution devolves upon theologians, and it is not necessary to see in the *assimilantur* of c. 368 more than what belongs there. C. 368 is a juridical text, not a theological text, and it should be interpreted according to c. 17 (the text and the context). And in this case, *assimilantur* (the text) is a term customarily used to express, in law, a formal comparison (as, for example, in c. 99); with respect to the context, c. 134 calls those communities *æquiparatæ*, whereby it is made clear that *assimilantur* is understood in its sense of *æquiparantur*; more indirectly, but just as clearly, c. 381 § 2 indicates that those who preside over those communities *in iure æquiparantur* to the diocesan bishop. In short, in juridical technique, it is not possible to distinguish between *assimilation* and *formal comparison*: they are the same thing. The word *assimilantur* is—as we said in the book—one of the several words whereby an *æquiparatio in iure* or formal comparison is established.[12]

7.   Formalism and Publicity

Formalism and publicity are two means used by the technique of law to protect security in the juridical order. Theoretically, because the juridical order i s a social system among persons, everything that works in the world of law should be external, meaning, it should be manifested externally. What is merely internal, not manifest, cannot be grasped by others and therefore cannot be the object of social relationships. Hence the importance of the sign in law as a necessary medium so that through it, what cannot be exteriorized by itself can be made manifest and be the object of social relationships and regulation. In this sense, the *form* or external figure by which something is known and can be grasped by others constitutes a primordial factor in law.

The forms are quite varied. An act of will may become manifest through words, silence, behavior or omission; it can be made manifest in writing or orally, using various means of expression, etc.

All forms or signs are not equally capable of expressing the content or intention of the things of which they are manifestations. This fact is an element of insecurity that may lead

---

12. Cf. J. I. ARRIETA, commentary to canon 368 in ExComCIC, vol. II/1 717–718; C. J. ERRÁZURIZ, "Circa l'equiparazione quale uso dell'analogia in diritto canonico," *Ius Ecclesiæ* IV [1992] 215–224; D. CENALMOR and J. MIRAS, *op. cit.*, note 6, 276–277.

to different and erroneous interpretations of the act or behavior. Thus arises the need to impose certain forms and formulas that in each case can best express the content, and the forms that are considered insufficient are discarded. Sometimes the forms and formulas are imposed by everyday usage; other times they are imposed by legislation. Selection of a single form may be based on prescription and be obligatory, but it does not exclude the juridical effects of other manifestations allowed (form *ad liceitatem*). Or it may also be held to be the only valid form when it is deemed that order and justice so demand (form *ad validitatem*).

Security is not, however, the only principle that justifies formalism in law. There is another basic factor to which we have alluded. Social relationships, facts and acts must be manifest. Furthermore, the only way people can communicate with one another is to capture the sign and the manifestation—in other words, the exterior figure that reveals another's intentions, thoughts and will. (This is so true that even in our relation with God, God's existence is grasped through his works, his will through signs and his deep truth through Revelation. Christ gives signals, which are the miracles, and manifests himself through his works. All this, evidently, is when God wishes to make contact with man in the *human mode*.) Thus law is dominated by the principle of form. Without manifestation there is no existence in the world of law. Furthermore, if this is correctly understood, we must speak of a certain predominance of form, in the sense that an act or behavior exists and is valid insofar as it is comprehensible by its sign or manifestation. Thus it is that any form and sign admitted is theoretically valid; that is, it results in an effect. In other words, any manifestation that is recognized produces at least an assumption of content. We say "at least" because sometimes security and justice require that a sign be absolutely valid.

If we look closely at reality we can see that principle of form is not specific to law, although its characteristics may be special. All of social life is colored by this principle. The importance of social forms is hidden from no one, even when they are disguised with a lack of form, which is nothing more than a different kind of formalization, many times louder and more formal than the forms an attempt is being made to eliminate. In another order of things, it is evident that personal faith is essentially "without form"; but when personal faith becomes manifest in or passes to a community, immediately a certain formalization appears: the formulas of the faith. In the Church, for example, the formulas—the Creed, conciliar canons, Magisterium, etc.—are not only words to facilitate expressing the faith in assemblies of worship, they are the *very expression of the content of the Church's faith.* And thus the truth contained in a formula is dogma. Of course, a formula has no absolute value, and it has none in law, except in the cases indicated and for the requirements of a just social order. Form in law appears as a sign or manifestation; thus it has an inherent reference to content. A sign is worth as much as the worth of what is expressed by the sign. That is why the predominance of form normally means nothing more than an assumption of content. Hence, for example, the relevance of simulation, error, etc., in juridical acts.

The principle of form touches the entire juridical order, including acts of authority. Acts of authority are expressed in forms and formulas; they are valid insofar as they are formalized and formulated, and they are interpreted in accordance with their forms. In perhaps no other field can this principle offer greater guarantees in defense of individual rights. In canon law this principle is well accepted with regard to the activity of the courts. Not so in legislative or administrative activities, with the consequent effect of insecurity in interpretation and the risk of arbitrariness in administrative bodies.

If formalism properly understood is a resource that favors the security of juridical traffic and to that degrees serves as a tool in defense of individual rights, when it is used to excess it results in a denaturing of the resource. Law then falls into a rigidity that suffocates the vital impulse of social reality. Excessive formalism is a sign of primitive or decadent law.

With regard to the principle of publicity, suffice it to say that all we have said about formalism is applicable here. In its specific aspects, publicity also obeys a basic reason and the principle of security in its deepest connotations.

Insofar as it must be external, every juridical act in some sense has a note of publicity. But when we speak of the principle of publicity in law, we refer in particular to certain means by which an act or a relationship or a juridical situation may be learned about by all interested parties. The means of publicizing are varied, from the intervention of public functionaries to the insertion of an announcement in the different communication media. Publicity or publication, depending on the case, can be a requirement *ad liceitatem*, or even *ad validitatem*. This principle is also especially applicable to norms, administrative acts and judicial decisions.

8. *Juridical Language*

In every science, language has a vital *raison d'être*. It is the vehicle for communicating and transmitting knowledge obtained. Its exact meaning is guaranteed to be understood insofar as possible, given the inherent limitations of language.

That is why juridical science uses its own language with a lexicon that in each case expresses—or should express—the concept, the judgment or the juridical consequences *precisely, clearly* and *simply*. Through the lexicon, normative imperatives are transmitted, judicial decisions are expressed or the content of juridical relationships is revealed.

Each concept requires a term to express it, and since juridical science creates its own typical concepts, it needs its own typical notional lexicon. Only such a lexicon can express juridical concepts without uncertainty or confusion.

It is not reasonable to expect laws or judicial decisions to use common language, clear and simple though it may be, and to avoid technical terms—making it into a language accessible to everyone. If this were the case, juridical language would lose precision and would be unable to express its content, or it would be necessary for laws to use long circumlocutions that would seriously harm their effectiveness. As Ihering said, a single technical expression saves a hundred words, and, we may add, it saves a hundred lawsuits.

In addition, a law is no place for fine discourses on the social importance of institutions nor for great exhortations. The purpose of a law is to organize social life effectively. For other purposes there are radio messages, encyclicals, pastoral letters or conciliar documents. A law is not an avant-garde ecclesiological essay.

However, the appropriate bodies do need the proper advisory services, and the faithful in general do need to know the law through publicizing efforts, when necessary.

Similarly, when we hear that laws should be drawn up in Biblical language, there is no other solution than to carry out a delicate didactical task and explain what law is. The same is true in the face of the opinion that laws should use a language reflecting certain subtle shades of the Christian attitude at the present time. Then the response must be that legislating or working in juridical science is not drawing up a will or a document to cause a good impression on any profane person that might read it; laws and science exist and are expressed in writing to resolve practical problems. Legislation or juridical science should reflect not language, but content: a just order suited to divine law, respectful, defender and guarantor of individual dignity and liberty, and an ecclesial system *in libertate filiorum Dei*.

The juridical lexicon is a tool of juridical technique. For that reason especially, it should be extremely *precise*. The purpose of law is to establish a stable order that can ensure all interests and needs for the common good, and it must effectively grasp social realities and contain them in systematic structures, while avoiding uncertainty and vagueness.

The use of common language, which is constantly subject to change and elastic meanings, would mean the immediate decay of law and its ordering force. Hence metaphors, symbols and *sui generis* expressions must be carefully avoided in juridical language, even though it does not always seem feasible; and it is not feasible precisely in cases where reality has not been captured in properly conceived terms or concepts.

The language used should also be *clear*; that is, it must be possible to capture the meaning, even if that is not always easy. Obscurity brings to social life nothing but a plurality of interpretations, synonymous with the ineffectiveness of laws. And in science, obscurity prevents the communication of results and sterilizes the task that has been accomplished.

Finally, the language must be *simple*, without unnecessary complications. Pomposity and complexity have no place in law, which is eminently functional, nor in science, which seeks the truth. Anything other than the sobriety proper to science or its technical tools is empty verbosity. As the American jurist Llewellyn says, the beauty of juridical language is a functional and efficient beauty.

9.   Basic Principles for Interpreting the Law

The most important nucleus of the juridical method is doubtless the set of rules and criteria for interpreting the law. Norms, juridical actions and administrative acts, to be applied, need to be interpreted. The juridical method, and the rules and technical resources for ordering social life, are made up of the criteria that serve to interpret the law. From a scientific point of view, this is the most interesting part of the method, because of its basic nature, for without interpretation there is no scientific knowledge, no systematic construction, no application to reality.

Not only the laws need to be interpreted; also custom, juridical actions and administrative acts and the whole juridical structure (rights, duties, etc.) need to be interpreted, and the rules for interpreting are peculiar to each case. That is why it is preferable to limit ourselves now to stating the basic principles of juridical interpretation and leave the presentation of the specific rules for the appropriate moment.

What does interpret mean? Interpretation of the law is commonly defined by canonists as a statement of the genuine meaning. The same can be said of interpreting custom, administrative acts or juridical actions. Theoretically, this is a perfectly valid definition, provided that interpretation is understood in its genuine form. Interpreting is, above all, an intellectual operation of understanding. It consists in grasping the *normative content* of law, the order that it is trying to implement, whether this is explicit in the law or not.

a) The first basic principle of interpretation is the connection between the juridical structure and social reality. Law is not a set of logical conclusions obtained by syllogisms from a priori principles. It is a system of and for social reality. It is a product of juridical prudence and as such must be constantly referred to in the situations of fact that it is trying to regulate. Juridical structure exists *as a function* of social reality. Its *raison d'être* is based on these two co-ordinates: a social reality that must be regulated, and the requirements of order and justice which the law and in general, juridical structure, claim to serve. If there is no social reality, there is no law properly speaking. It is either a historic relic or a pure intellectual game. What else could a law be that in the present time claimed, for example, to regulate fiefdoms? And if there are no order and justice requirements, regulation escapes the nature and function of law.

Although social reality presents a whole range of possibilities for being organized into something upon which legislative options are based, it has a fundamental nucleus of inherent order. It has a nucleus of normativity, because all of reality naturally has a sense and direction. The normative content of all juridical structures should be understood as a function of and in relation to social reality and its fundamental nucleus of normativity; it should be a function of the necessities and demands of order and justice. In this way it is not correct to interpret law only through its statements without taking into account social reality at the same time.

b) Directly tied to the first general principle is the second principle, the historicity of law. The essential and inherently practical dimension (an effective and living order) of law implies that juridical structures should be interpreted in accordance with their moment in history, and we are not speaking now of adaptation. Interpretation of the law generally has an undercurrent of ideas that influence it, often decisively. A given law, for example, may be understood— interpreted— with different shades of meaning depending upon the mentality with which it is viewed. Social reality, immersed in history, acquires new shades of meaning with the passing of time. The law should always be interpreted in relation to its historical dimension, meaning current times.

c) Finally, a basic and very fundamental criterion is the *meaning* or *purpose of law*. A given juridical structure, a norm, a right, a duty, etc. is not fully expressed in the immediate purpose that appears in its statement. These elements are only aspects, factors or parts of a broader and more complete order of things that should be reflected in their interpretation. Each of a parish priest's or bishop's functions, for example, is not fully understood unless seen in its proper pastoral function; each marriage right is a function of the purposes of marriage; ecclesiastical property has specific objectives, etc. Thus, all norms or elements of a juridical structure have a *meaning* that is fuller than when taken alone. This *meaning* is a factor of the first order for interpreting them, for understanding their nature, delimiting their scope and strength, and understanding their purpose.

In conclusion, the law must be interpreted realistically, with a sense of the moment in time and using teleological criteria.

Last published / Dernières publications

HANDBOOKS / MANUELS

Introduction to the Study of Canon Law, J. HERVADA, 2007, ISBN 978-2-89127-836-2.

A Handbook on Canon Law, 2nd updated edition, J. T. MARTÍN DE AGAR, 2007, ISBN 978-2-89127-804-1.

Liturgie et droit – Le droit liturgique dans le système du droit canonique de l'Église catholique, John HUELS, Traduit par Jean PELLETIER, 2007, ISBN 978-2-89127-811-9.

NOTEBOOKS / CAHIERS

The Juridical Mind of Saint Josemaria Escriva, A Brief History of the Canonical Path of Opus Dei, 2nd updated edition, 2007, E. CAPARROS, ISBN 978-2-89127-833-1.

La mentalité juridique de saint Josémaria Escriva. Un bref historique de l'itinéraire canonique de l'Opus Dei, E. CAPARROS, 2007, ISBN 9778-2-89127-834-8.

RESEARCH TOOLS / INSTRUMENTS DE RECHERCHE

Dictionnaire biographique des cardinaux du XIXᵉ siècle, Jean LEBLANC, 2007, ISBN 978-2-89127-801-0.

ANNOTATED LEGISLATIVE TEXTS / TEXTES LÉGISLATIFS ANNOTÉS

Code de droit canonique bilingue et annoté (3ᵉ éd.), E. CAPARROS, H. AUBÉ (directeurs), 2007, ISBN 978-2-89127-768-6.

Forthcoming / En préparation

HANDBOOKS / MANUELS

Introduction to the History of the Sources of Canon Law I – The Ancient Law up to the Decretum of Gratian, Brian E. FERME, 2007, ISBN 978-2-89127-805-8.

NOTEBOOKS / CAHIERS

Fidèles dans le monde. La sécularité des laïcs chrétiens, Jorge MIRAS, 2007, ISBN 978-2-89127-841-6.

Published in 2006 / Parus en 2006

PROCEEDINGS / ACTES

Symposium on Dignitas connubii, Patricia M. DUGAN & Luis NAVARRO (Editors), 2006, ISBN 2-89127-782-1.

ANNOTATED LEGISLATIVE TEXTS / TEXTES LÉGISLATIFS ANNOTÉS

Canonical and Pastoral Guide for Parishes, Canadian Edition, Assembly of Catholic Bishops of Québec; J. PELLETIER (Editor), 2006, ISBN 2-89127-779-1.

Guide canonique et pastoral au service des paroisses. Édition canadienne, Assemblée des évêques catholiques du Québec; J. PELLETIER (directeur), 2006, ISBN 2-89127-778-3.

HANDBOOKS / MANUELS

A Critical Introduction to Natural Law, J. HERVADA, 2006, ISBN 2-89127-776-7.

Advocacy Vademecum, Patricia M. DUGAN (Editor), 2006, ISBN 2-89127-777-5.

Liturgy and Law – Liturgical Law in the System of Roman Catholic Canon Law, J. M. HUELS, 2006, ISBN 2-89127-773-2.

Other published / Déjà parus

Canonical and Pastoral Guide for Parishes, Assembly of Bishops of Québec; J. PELLETIER (Editor), 2005, ISBN 2-89127-640-X.

Incrementa in Progressu 1983 Codicis Iuris Canonici with a Multilingual Introduction (English, Français, Italiano, Español, Deutsch, Polski), E. N. PETERS, 2005, ISBN 2-89127-663-7.

The Penal Process and the Protection of Rights in Canon Law, Patricia M. DUGAN (Editor), 2005, ISBN 2-89127-664-7.

Code of Canon Law Annotated, 2nd revised and updated edition, E. CAPARROS, H. AUBÉ (Editors), 2004, International edition, MTF ISBN 1-890177-44-X/Canadian edition W&L, ISBN 2-89127-629-9.

Exegetical Commentary on the Code of Canon Law; Á. MARZOA, J. MIRAS, R. RODRÍGUEZ-OCAÑA (Editors); E. CAPARROS (General Editor, English edition).

International edition 2004:
- Volume I Chicago, MTF ISBN 1-890177-34-2/Montréal, W&L, ISBN 2-89127-621-3
- Volume II/1 Chicago, MTF ISBN 1-890177-35-0/Montréal, W&L, ISBN 2-89127-622-1
- Volume II/2 Chicago, MTF ISBN 1-890177-36-9/Montréal, W&L, ISBN 2-89127-623-X
- Volume III/1 Chicago, MTF ISBN 1-890177-37-7/Montréal, W&L, ISBN 2-89127-624-8
- Volume III/2 Chicago, MTF ISBN 1-890177-38-5/Montréal, W&L, ISBN 2-89127-625-6
- Volume IV/1 Chicago, MTF ISBN 1-890177-39-3/Montréal, W&L, ISBN 2-89127-626-4
- Volume IV/2 Chicago, MTF ISBN 1-890177-40-7/Montréal, W&L, ISBN 2-89127-627-2
- Volume V Chicago, MTF ISBN 1-890177-41-5/Montréal, W&L, ISBN 2-89127-628-0

Guide canonique et pastoral au service des paroisses II, Assemblée des évêques du Québec, J. PELLETIER (directeur), 2004 ISBN 2-89127-639-6.

Code de droit canonique bilingue et annoté (2ᵉ éd.), E. CAPARROS, M. THÉRIAULT, J. THORN (†) (directeurs), 1999, 2ᵉ tirage 2003; ISBN 2-89127-460-1.

Dictionnaire biographique des évêques catholiques du Canada (1658-2002), J. LEBLANC, 2002, ISBN 2-89127-506-8.

Code of Canon Law Annotated, E. CAPARROS, M. THÉRIAULT, J. THORN (Editors), 1st edition: March 1993, 2nd printing: October 1993, 3rd printing: 1996, 4th printing: 1997, 5th printing: 2000, ISBN 2-89127-232-3 (out of print).

Governance Structures Within the Catholic Church, J. I. ARRIETA, 2000, ISBN 2-89127-518-7.

Tabulæ congruentiæ inter Codicem iuris canonici et versiones anteriores canonum: With a Multilingual Introduction (English, Français, Italiano, Español, Deutsch), E. N. PETERS, 2000, ISBN 2-89127-500-4.

A Handbook on Canon Law, J. T. MARTÍN DE AGAR, 1999, ISBN 2-89127-457-1.

La charge pastorale d'une paroisse sans curé, B. A. CUSAK & T. G. SULLIVAN, trad. et adaptation par M. THÉRIAULT, 1997, ISBN 2-89127-417-2.

Code de droit canonique, E. CAPARROS, M. THÉRIAULT, J. THORN (directeurs), édition bilingue et annotée, 1ʳᵉ édition : mars 1990, 2ᵉ tirage : décembre 1990, 3ᵉ tirage : 1994, 4ᵉ tirage : 1995, ISBN 2-89127-153-X (épuisé).

NCCB/Conférence des évêques catholiques des États-Unis. Le manuel de l'évêque, trad. par M. THÉRIAULT, 1994, ISBN 2-89127-309-5 (épuisé).

Orders to / Commander à:

| WILSON & LAFLEUR LTÉE

40, Notre-Dame Est
Montréal (Québec) Canada H2Y 1B9
Tél. : 514 875-6326 / 1 800 363-2327 • Téléc. : 514 875-8356
www.wilsonlafleur.com

| USA

www.CanonLawBooks.com
2662 East Allegheny Avenue
Philadelphia, PA 19134-5115
Phone: 215 634-2355 • Fax: 215 634-2373

| EUROPE

Éditions Le Laurier
19, passage Jean Nicot
75007 PARIS
Tél. : +33 1.45.51.55.08 • Fax : +33 1.45.51.81.83
e-mail : editions@lelaurier.fr
www.lelaurier.fr

Midwest Theological Forum
1420 Davey Road
Woodridge, IL 60517 U.S.A
Phone: 630 739-9750 • Fax: 630 739-9758
e-mail: mail@mwtf.org